SARDINIA
Guide 2024

Sardinia for First-Timers:
Everything You Need to Know to
Plan the Perfect Trip

By

Walter Tour

Copyright All rights reserved. No part of this publication may be reproduced, distributed, or transmitted in any form or by any means, including photocopying, recording, or other electronic or mechanical methods, without the prior written permission of the publisher, except in the case of brief quotations embodied in critical reviews and certain other noncommercial uses permitted by copyright law.

Copyright © Walter Tour, 2023

Table of Contents

Chapter 1: Sardinia Essentials 9
    Introduction to Sardinia 9
    Best Time to Visit 11
    Travel Documentation and Visas 12
    Currency, Money, and Budgeting 15
Chapter 2: Getting to Sardinia 20
    Air Travel to Sardinia 20
        Major Airports and Airlines 20
        Booking Tips and Hacks 23
        Airport Facilities 25
        Transportation to the City 28
    Sea Travel to Sardinia 30
        Ferry Routes and Operators 30
        Booking and Boarding Process 33
        Tips for Booking and Boarding Ferries 35
        Onboarld Services 37
        Port Cities and Arrivals 41
Chapter 3: Navigating Sardinia's Regions 44
    Coastal Explorations 44
        Costa Smeralda: Glamour and Luxury 44
        Costa Paradiso: Rugged Beauty 47

Oristano Beaches: Tranquil Escapes 50
Sardinia's Eastern Coast: Hidden Gems 52
Inland Adventures 55
Barbagia Region: Heart of Sardinia 55
Gennargentu National Park: Hiking Paradise 59
Traditional Villages and Culture 62
Nuragic Sites: Ancient Wonders 66
Chapter 4: Sardinian Culture and Traditions 69
Festivals and Celebrations 69
Sa Sartiglia: Carnival in Oristano 69
Traditional Sardinian Dress 72
Craftsmanship and Artistry 75
Sardinian Cuisine 79
Local Culinary Traditions 79
MustTry Dishes and Desserts 83
Wines and Liquors 87
Dining Etiquette 90
Chapter 5: MustSee Cities and Towns 95
Cagliari: The Capital 95
Historic Districts and Landmarks 95
Local Culture and Cuisine 98
Day Trips from Cagliari 102
Alghero: Catalan Influence 104

Alghero's Old Town...104

Beaches and Waterfront 108

Olbia: Gateway to Costa Smeralda............................112

Introduction to Olbia...112

Luxury Resorts..116

Beaches, Dining, and Nightlife..............................119

Excursions and Boat Tours 121

Chapter 6: Natural Paradise...125

Water Sports and Activities[00] 125

Beach Clubs and Relaxation 129

Hiking and Trekking Adventures 132

Supramonte Mountains 132

Monte Limbara: Alpine Escape.........................137

Flora and Fauna..140

Adventure Sports 143

Chapter 7: Exploring Sardinia's History.....................149

Nuragic Civilization 149

Nuraghe Structures...149

Archeological Sites 152

Museums and Exhibitions................................157

Medieval and Historic Landmarks.........................162

Castles and Fortresses.......................................162

Sardinian Architecture 172

Chapter 8: Sardinia for Food Enthusiasts 178
   Sardinian Cuisine..178
      Sardinian Ingredients and Flavors 178
      Regional Specialties...181
      Markets and Food Tours..183
   Dining Recommendations 187
      Fine Dining..187
      Street Food 194
      Sardinian Desserts and Sweets 197

Chapter 9: Practical Tips for Travelers........................202
   Accommodations and Lodging 202
      Hotels, Resorts, and Agriturismos.......................202
      Accommodation Etiquette.....................................211
      Alternative Stays 215
   Language and Communication 218
      Useful Phrases and Words....................................218
   Communication Tips..223
      Language Resources 223
      Local Dialects..226

Chapter 10: Sardinia Dos and Don'ts 230
   Respect for Local Customs.......................................230
   Environmental Responsibility 233
   Safety and Health Tips 236

Souvenirs and Mementos 241

Chapter 1: Sardinia Essentials

Introduction to Sardinia

Nestled in the embrace of the crystal-clear Mediterranean Sea, Sardinia beckons to travelers with its enchanting beauty and timeless allure. This Italian gem, often described as a paradise on Earth, is a destination that awakens the senses and leaves an indelible mark on the heart.

As you set foot on this island, you'll be greeted by a land steeped in history, where ancient ruins whisper stories of civilizations long past. Yet, Sardinia isn't just a place of the past – it's a living tapestry of culture, tradition, and warmth. The locals, proud of their heritage, welcome visitors with open arms and share the island's rich traditions, from music and dance to the mouthwatering flavors of their cuisine.

The landscape of Sardinia is a masterpiece of nature. Pristine beaches with powdery white sand and turquoise waters stretch as far as the eye can see. Rugged cliffs and dramatic coastlines create a stark contrast to the serene countryside, where olive groves and vineyards flourish. Inland, the rugged beauty of the Gennargentu Mountains invites explorers to delve into the heart of the island.

But Sardinia's magic doesn't end with its landscapes and culture; it continues beneath the waves. The island's seas are a haven for divers and snorkelers, boasting an underwater world teeming with colorful marine life and ancient shipwrecks.

Sardinia is a destination that promises both relaxation and adventure. Whether you seek tranquility on a pristine beach or wish to explore its vibrant history, the island offers something for everyone. So, as you embark on your journey to Sardinia, prepare to be captivated by a place where time stands still, and where every moment becomes a page in your own unique travel story.

Best Time to Visit

Sardinia is a beautiful Mediterranean island with something to offer visitors year-round. However, the best time to visit depends on your interests and what you want to get out of your trip.

Summer (June-August) is the peak tourist season in Sardinia, and for good reason. The weather is warm and sunny, the beaches are packed with people, and there are festivals and events happening all over the island. However, it's important to note that Sardinia can be very crowded and expensive during this time of year.

Spring (April-May) and autumn (September-October) are great shoulder seasons to visit Sardinia. The weather is still mild, but there are fewer crowds and lower prices. This is a good time to visit if you're interested in hiking, biking, or exploring the island's many cultural attractions.

Winter (November-March) is the off-season in Sardinia, and it's the best time to visit if you're on a budget or prefer to avoid the crowds. The weather can be unpredictable during this time of year, but there are still plenty of things to see and do, such as visiting museums, exploring historical sites, and enjoying the island's natural beauty.

Here is a more detailed breakdown of the best time to visit Sardinia, depending on your interests:

- Beaches: June-September

- Hiking and biking: April-May and September-October

- Cultural attractions: April-May, September-October, and November-March

- Festivals and events: June-August

- Budget travel: November-March

Travel Documentation and Visas

Sardinia is a beautiful Mediterranean island with something to offer visitors year-round. Its stunning beaches, crystal-clear waters, and rugged mountains make it a popular tourist destination. However, it's important to make sure you have the proper travel documentation and visa before you go.

Entry Requirements

Sardinia is part of Italy, so all visitors must have a valid passport. If you are a citizen of a visa-exempt country, you can stay in Sardinia for up to 90 days within a 180-day period without a visa. However, if you are not a citizen of a visa-exempt country, you will need to apply for a Schengen visa.

Schengen Visas

A Schengen visa is a visa that allows you to travel freely within the Schengen Area, which includes 26 European countries, including Italy. To apply for a Schengen visa, you will need to visit the Italian embassy or consulate in your home country. You will need to provide your passport, a visa application form, two passport-sized photos, proof of travel insurance, and proof of accommodation in Sardinia.

Other Travel Documentation

Note: you may also want to bring the following travel documentation with you to Sardinia:

- **Return or onward ticket**: This shows that you have a plan to leave Sardinia within the permitted timeframe.

- **Proof of accommodation:** This is especially important if you are traveling during the peak season.

- **Travel insurance:** This is essential in case of any unexpected events, such as lost luggage or medical emergencies.

- **European Health Insurance Card (EHIC):** This card gives you access to state-provided healthcare in Italy.

Tips for Getting Your Visa

Here are a few tips for getting your Schengen visa:

- Apply for your visa well in advance of your trip. It can take up to several weeks to process a visa application.

- Make sure you have all of the required documentation before you apply.

- Fill out the visa application form carefully and completely.

- Be prepared to answer questions about your travel plans.

Traveling to Sardinia with Children

If you are traveling to Sardinia with children, they will also need to have a valid passport. If they are under the age of 18 and traveling with only one parent or guardian, they will need a letter of consent from the other parent or guardian.

Currency, Money, and Budgeting

Currency

The official currency of Sardinia is the euro (EUR). Euro coins and banknotes are accepted throughout the island. However, it's always a good idea to have some cash on hand, especially if you're planning on visiting smaller villages or markets.

Money Exchange

You can exchange money at banks, currency exchange bureaus, and hotels. However, it's important to compare exchange rates before you exchange your money. Banks typically offer the best exchange rates, but they may charge a commission fee. Currency exchange bureaus and hotels may offer less competitive exchange rates, but they may not charge a commission fee.

Credit and Debit Cards

Credit and debit cards are widely accepted in Sardinia, but it's always a good idea to have some cash on hand, especially if you're planning on visiting smaller villages or markets. It's also important to note that some businesses may charge a surcharge for credit card transactions.

ATMs

ATMs are widely available in Sardinia, but they may not be available in smaller villages or markets. It's always a good idea to check with your bank to see if your ATM card will work in Italy.

Budgeting

Sardinia can be an expensive island, especially during the peak season. However, there are ways to budget for your trip. Here are a few tips:

- **Cook your own meals:** Eating out can be expensive in Sardinia. Save money by cooking your own meals. There are many grocery stores on the island where you can buy fresh produce and other food items.

- **Stay in hostels or guesthouses:** Accommodation costs can be high in Sardinia, especially during the peak season. Save money by staying in hostels or guesthouses. There are many affordable options available throughout the island.

- **Take advantage of free activities:** There are many free things to do in Sardinia, such as swimming at the beach, hiking in the mountains, and visiting museums.

- **Use public transportation:** Renting a car can be expensive in Sardinia. Save money by using public transportation. There is a bus service that connects all of the major towns and villages on the island.

Here is a sample budget for a week-long trip to Sardinia:

Accommodation: €300-€500 Food: €200-€300 Activities: €100-€200 Transportation: €50-€100

Total: €650-€1,100

This budget is just a starting point. You may need to adjust it depending on your travel style and budget.

Here are a few additional tips for saving money in Sardinia:

- **Avoid eating at tourist traps:** Restaurants in popular tourist areas tend to be more expensive. Save money by eating at restaurants in less touristy areas.

- **Ask for discounts:** Many businesses in Sardinia offer discounts for students, seniors, and military personnel. Be sure to ask about discounts before you make a purchase.

- **Take advantage of free Wi-Fi:** Many hotels, restaurants, and cafes offer free Wi-Fi. Save money by using free Wi-Fi whenever possible.

- **Travel during the shoulder season:** Sardinia is less expensive during the shoulder season (April-May and September-

October). If you can, try to travel during this time of year.

Chapter 2: Getting to Sardinia

Air Travel to Sardinia

Major Airports and Airlines

Major Airports

Sardinia has three major airports:

- Cagliari Elmas Airport (CAG): This is the largest airport on the island and is located about 4 miles from the city of Cagliari.

- Olbia Costa Smeralda Airport (OLB): This airport is located about 4 miles from the city of Olbia and is popular with tourists visiting the Costa Smeralda region.

- Alghero-Fertilia Airport (AHO): This airport is located about 8 miles from the city of Alghero and is popular with tourists visiting the northwestern part of the island.

All three airports are well-connected to major cities throughout Europe and Italy.

Airlines

A number of airlines fly to Sardinia, including:

- ITA Airways
- Alitalia
- Ryanair
- EasyJet
- Vueling
- British Airways
- Lufthansa
- Air France
- KLM
- Iberia
- SWISS

- Eurowings

Arriving at the Airport

- Once you arrive at the airport, you'll need to go through passport control and customs.

- If you're renting a car, you can pick it up at the airport.

- If you're taking a taxi or bus, you'll find them outside the airport terminal.

Getting from the Airport to Your Resort

- The best way to get from the airport to your resort depends on where you're staying.

- If you're staying in a major tourist area, such as the Costa Smeralda, there will be a regular bus service from the airport.

- If you're staying in a more remote location, you may need to take a taxi or rent a car.

Tips for Enjoying Your Air Travel to Sardinia

- Arrive at the airport at least two hours before your flight is scheduled to depart.

- Bring a book or magazine to keep yourself entertained on the flight.

- Drink plenty of water to stay hydrated.

- If you're traveling with children, bring some snacks and activities to keep them occupied.

Booking Tips and Hacks

Sardinia is a beautiful island in the Mediterranean Sea that is popular with tourists from all over the world. The island has stunning beaches, crystal-clear waters, and rugged mountains. However, Sardinia can also be an expensive island to visit, especially during the peak season. Here are a few booking tips and hacks to help you save money on your trip to Sardinia:

- Book your flights and accommodation in advance. This is especially important if you're traveling during the peak season (June-August).

- Consider flying into a smaller airport. Cagliari Elmas Airport (CAG) is the largest airport on the island, but it can be more expensive to fly into. Consider flying into a smaller airport, such as Olbia Costa Smeralda Airport (OLB) or Alghero-Fertilia Airport (AHO), if you're planning on staying in the northeastern or northwestern parts of the island, respectively.

- Choose budget-friendly accommodation. There are a variety of budget-friendly accommodation options available in Sardinia, such as hostels, guesthouses, and self-catering apartments.

- Eat at local restaurants. Avoid eating at tourist traps, which tend to be more expensive. Instead, eat at local restaurants where you can enjoy authentic Sardinian cuisine at reasonable prices.

- Take advantage of free activities. There are many free things to do in Sardinia, such as swimming at the beach, hiking in the mountains, and visiting museums.

Here are a few additional booking hacks to help you save money on your trip to Sardinia:

- Use a travel search engine to compare prices from different airlines and travel websites.

- Look for deals and discounts. Many airlines and hotels offer deals and discounts throughout the year.

- Consider traveling during the shoulder season. The shoulder season (April-May and September-October) is a great time to visit Sardinia, as the crowds are smaller and the prices are lower.

- Book your tours and activities in advance. This is especially important if you're planning on visiting popular attractions, such as the Costa Smeralda or the Maddalena Archipelago.

- Negotiate prices with taxi drivers and tour operators. Sardinia is a very competitive market, so don't be afraid to negotiate prices with taxi drivers and tour operators.

Airport Facilities

The three major airports in Sardinia - Cagliari Elmas Airport (CAG), Olbia Costa Smeralda Airport (OLB), and Alghero-Fertilia Airport (AHO) - offer a variety of facilities and services for passengers.

General Facilities

All three airports have the following facilities:

- Arrival and departure halls
- Check-in and baggage drop-off areas
- Passport control and customs
- Security checkpoints
- Gates for boarding and disembarking aircraft
- Information desks
- ATMs
- Currency exchange bureaus
- Restaurants and cafes

- Shops

- Free Wi-Fi

Some of the additional facilities available at the three major airports in Sardinia include:

- Cagliari Elmas Airport: Business center, conference room, VIP lounge, prayer room, first aid center, pharmacy, lost and found office, car rental desks, taxis, buses

- Olbia Costa Smeralda Airport: Nursery and baby club, VIP lounge, prayer room, first aid center, pharmacy, lost and found office, car rental desks, taxis, buses

- Alghero-Fertilia Airport: VIP lounge, prayer room, first aid center, pharmacy, lost and found office, car rental desks, taxis, buses

Facilities for Passengers with Disabilities

All three airports in Sardinia are accessible to passengers with disabilities. There are elevators, ramps, and accessible restrooms throughout the airports. Wheelchairs and assistance can be requested at the information desks.

Tips for Using the Airport Facilities

- Arrive at the airport at least two hours before your flight is scheduled to depart. This will give you enough time to check in, go through security, and find your gate.

- If you have a lot of luggage, you may want to consider using a luggage trolley.

- Take advantage of the free Wi-Fi to stay connected with friends and family.1

- If you need assistance, don't be afraid to ask at the information desks.

Transportation to the City

There are a few different ways to get to the city from the airports in Sardinia:

Taxi

The fastest and most convenient way to get to the city from the airport is by taxi. Taxis are available outside the airport terminals and can be taken to any destination in Sardinia. The taxi ride from Cagliari Elmas Airport to the city center takes about 15 minutes and costs around €25. The taxi ride from Olbia Costa Smeralda Airport to the city center takes about 30 minutes and costs around €40. The taxi ride from Alghero-Fertilia Airport to the city center takes about 10 minutes and costs around €20.

Bus

There is a regular bus service from all three airports to the city centers. The bus ride from Cagliari Elmas Airport to the city center takes about 30 minutes and costs around €1.30. The bus ride from Olbia Costa Smeralda Airport to the city center takes about 45 minutes and costs around €2.00. The bus ride from Alghero-Fertilia Airport to the city center takes about 20 minutes and costs around €1.50.

Train

There is a train station at Cagliari Elmas Airport that offers service to the city center and other destinations in Sardinia. The train ride from

Cagliari Elmas Airport to the city center takes about 10 minutes and costs around €1.30.

Car rental

If you are planning on staying in Sardinia for more than a few days, you may want to consider renting a car. This will give you the flexibility to explore the island at your own pace. There are car rental desks at all three airports.

Tips for Getting to the City from the Airport

- If you are taking a taxi, be sure to agree on a price with the driver before you get in the car.

- If you are taking the bus, be sure to check the bus schedule in advance.

- If you are taking the train, be sure to purchase your tickets in advance.

- If you are renting a car, be sure to book it in advance, especially if you are traveling during the peak season.

Sea Travel to Sardinia

Ferry Routes and Operators

Sardinia is a beautiful island in the Mediterranean Sea, and there are many ways to get there. One of the most popular ways to travel to Sardinia is by ferry. Ferries depart from several ports in Italy and France, and there are a variety of ferry companies to choose from.

Ferry Routes

The following ferry routes are available to Sardinia:

- Italy: Civitavecchia, Genoa, Livorno, Piombino, Porto Torres, Olbia, Golfo Aranci, Cagliari
- France: Nice, Toulon, Bonifacio

Ferry Operators

The following ferry companies operate ferries to Sardinia:

- Grimaldi Lines

- Moby Lines
- Tirrenia
- Corsica Ferries
- Ichnusa Lines
- GNV

When to Book Your Ferry

It is important to book your ferry tickets in advance, especially if you are traveling during the peak season (June-August). Ferry tickets can be booked online or through a travel agent.

What to Bring on the Ferry

Be sure to bring the following items on the ferry:

- Passport or ID
- Ferry tickets
- Food and drinks

- Entertainment (books, magazines, games, etc.)

- A jacket or sweater (the ferry can be cool at night)

- Sunscreen (if you are traveling during the summer)

Tips for Enjoying Your Ferry Ride

- Arrive at the ferry port at least two hours before your ferry is scheduled to depart.

- Check in for your ferry at the counter and receive your boarding pass.

- Board the ferry and find your seat or cabin.

- Relax and enjoy the views!

Booking and Boarding Process

Booking

There are two main ways to book ferry tickets:

- **Online**: This is the most convenient way to book ferry tickets, and it is often the cheapest option as well. Most ferry companies have websites where you can book your tickets online.

- **Through a travel agent:** If you are not comfortable booking your ferry tickets online, you can book them through a travel agent. Travel agents may charge a fee for their services, but they can help you find the best deal on ferry tickets and they can also help you book your other travel arrangements, such as flights and accommodation.

Once you have chosen your ferry route and date, you will need to enter your personal information and payment details. You will also need to choose the type of ticket you want to purchase. There are a variety of ticket options available, such as one-way tickets, round-trip tickets, and tickets that include accommodation on the ferry.

Boarding

On the day of your ferry ride, you will need to arrive at the ferry port at least two hours before your ferry is scheduled to depart. This will give you enough time to check in, go through security, and find your gate.

To check in for your ferry, you will need to present your passport or ID and your ferry tickets to the counter staff. The counter staff will give you your boarding pass.

Once you have your boarding pass, you can go through security. Security checks are similar to airport security checks. You will need to remove your shoes and belt and you will need to place your luggage in an X-ray machine.

After you have gone through security, you can find your gate. The gate number will be printed on your boarding pass.

When you are ready to board the ferry, the gate staff will scan your boarding pass. Once you have boarded the ferry, you can find your seat or cabin.

Tips for Booking and Boarding Ferries

Here are a few tips for booking and boarding ferries:

- Book your ferry tickets in advance, especially if you are traveling during the peak season.

- Compare prices from different ferry companies before you book your tickets.

- Choose the type of ticket that is right for you. Consider factors such as the length of your trip, the type of accommodation you want, and your budget.

- Arrive at the ferry port at least two hours before your ferry is scheduled to depart.

- Check in for your ferry at the counter and receive your boarding pass.

- Go through security.

- Find your gate.

- Have your boarding pass scanned when you board the ferry.

- Find your seat or cabin.

Here are a few additional tips for booking and boarding ferries:

- If you are traveling with a car, be sure to book your car space on the ferry in advance.

- If you are traveling with pets, be sure to check the ferry company's policy on pets.

- If you have any special needs, be sure to contact the ferry company in advance.

- If you are traveling during the summer, be sure to bring sunscreen, a hat, and sunglasses.

- If you are traveling during the winter, be sure to bring a jacket or sweater.

- Enjoy the ride!

Onboarld Services

Ferries offer a variety of onboard services to keep passengers entertained and comfortable during their journey. The specific services offered will vary depending on the ferry company and the length of the journey, but some common onboard services include:

Food and Drink

Most ferries have a restaurant or cafeteria where passengers can purchase food and drinks. The type of food and drinks available will vary depending on the ferry company, but some common options include burgers, pizzas, sandwiches, salads, and snacks. Some ferries also have bars where passengers can purchase alcoholic and non-alcoholic beverages.

Entertainment

Many ferries offer entertainment options for passengers, such as movies, TV shows, live music, and video games. Some ferries also have children's play areas and arcades.

Shopping

Some ferries have shops where passengers can purchase souvenirs, snacks, and other items. The types of items available will vary depending on the ferry company, but some common items include clothing, hats, sunglasses, and souvenirs.

Internet Access

Many ferries offer internet access to passengers for a fee. The speed and reliability of the internet access will vary depending on the ferry company and the location of the ferry.

Other Services

Other onboard services that may be available include:

- Currency exchange
- ATMs
- First aid
- Prayer rooms
- Business centers

- Conference rooms

- VIP lounges

Tips for Enjoying Onboard Services

Here are a few tips for enjoying onboard services:

- Check the ferry company's website in advance to see what onboard services are available.

- Bring cash with you in case the ferry does not have ATMs or accept credit cards.

- If you are traveling with children, be sure to check the ferry company's policy on children's activities.

- If you have any special needs, be sure to contact the ferry company in advance.

- Relax and enjoy the ride!

- If you are traveling with a group, consider booking a table at the restaurant in advance.

- If you are planning on using the internet, be sure to purchase an internet access pass in advance.

- If you are traveling with children, be sure to take advantage of the children's activities.

- If you have any dietary restrictions, be sure to let the restaurant staff know.

- If you are celebrating a special occasion, be sure to let the ferry company know so that they can make arrangements.

Port Cities and Arrivals

Port cities are bustling hubs of activity, where ships from all over the world arrive and depart carrying goods and people. These cities are often home to a diverse range of cultures and languages, and they play a vital role in the global economy.

Port cities are often vibrant and cosmopolitan places, with a rich history and culture. They are also home to a diverse range of attractions, from museums and art galleries to restaurants and nightlife.

Here are some of the things you can do in some of the world's busiest port cities:

- **Shanghai**: Visit the Bund, a waterfront promenade with stunning views of the city skyline; explore the Yu Garden, a classical Chinese garden; or take a walk through Fuxing Park, a popular spot for locals and tourists alike.

- **Singapore**: Visit the Gardens by the Bay, a futuristic park with giant Supertree Grove and Cloud Forest and Flower Dome conservatories; explore the Chinatown and Little India neighborhoods; or take a ride on the Singapore Flyer, the world's tallest Ferris wheel.

- **Ningbo-Zhoushan**: Visit the Tianyi Pavilion, the oldest library in China; explore the Hemudu Site, a Neolithic village; or take a boat trip to the Thousand Islands, a group of over 3,000 islands.

- **Shenzhen**: Visit the Window of the World, a theme park with replicas of famous landmarks from around the world; explore the Splendid China Folk Culture Village, a miniature park with traditional Chinese architecture from different regions; or take a ferry to Hong Kong.

- **Guangzhou**: Visit the Chen Clan Ancestral Hall, a UNESCO World Heritage Site; explore the Shamian Island, a former European concession with colonial architecture; or take a boat trip on the Pearl River.

These are just a few of the many things you can do in the world's busiest port cities. With their diverse cultures, vibrant attractions, and global economies, these cities are sure to offer something for everyone.

Chapter 3: Navigating Sardinia's Regions

Coastal Explorations

Costa Smeralda: Glamour and Luxury

The Costa Smeralda, or Emerald Coast, is a stretch of coastline in northeastern Sardinia that is known for its stunning beaches, crystal-clear waters, and luxurious resorts. It is a popular destination for celebrities, jet-setters, and those who simply want to experience the best that life has to offer.

The Costa Smeralda was developed in the 1960s by Prince Karim Aga Khan IV, who envisioned creating a destination that would rival the French Riviera. He invited some of the world's most famous architects and designers to create resorts and villas that would blend in with the natural beauty of the area.

The result is a coastal paradise that is dotted with picturesque villages, world-class golf courses, and exclusive marinas. The beaches are some of the most beautiful in the world, with white sand and turquoise waters. The waters are also crystal clear, making them ideal for swimming, snorkeling, and diving.

The Costa Smeralda is home to a number of luxury resorts, including the Hotel Cala di Volpe, the Hotel Porto Cervo, and the Hotel Pitrizza. These resorts offer guests the ultimate in luxury and relaxation, with private beaches, swimming pools, tennis courts, and golf courses.

The Costa Smeralda is also known for its vibrant nightlife. There are a number of bars and clubs in the area where guests can enjoy a night out on the town.

If you are looking for a coastal destination that offers stunning scenery, luxurious accommodations, and a vibrant nightlife, then the Costa Smeralda is the perfect place for you.

Things to do in the Costa Smeralda:

- **Visit the Porto Cervo marina:** Porto Cervo is the main town in the Costa Smeralda and it is home to a number of luxury yachts and boutiques.

- **Relax on the beach:** The Costa Smeralda is home to some of the most beautiful beaches in the world. Some of the most popular beaches include Cala di Volpe, Spiaggia Grande, and Cala Longa.

- **Play a round of golf:** The Costa Smeralda is home to a number of world-class golf courses, including the Pevero Golf Club and the Is Molas Golf Club.

- **Go shopping:** The Costa Smeralda is home to a number of luxury boutiques, where you can find everything from designer clothes to jewelry to home decor.

- **Enjoy the nightlife**: The Costa Smeralda has a vibrant nightlife scene, with a number of bars and clubs where you can enjoy a night out on the town.

Tips for visiting the Costa Smeralda:

- **Book your accommodations in advance**: The Costa Smeralda is a popular destination, so it is important to book your accommodations well in advance, especially if you are traveling during the peak season (June-August).

- **Pack for all types of weather:** The weather in the Costa Smeralda can be unpredictable, so it is important to pack for all types of weather. Be sure to bring a jacket or sweater, as well as sunscreen and sunglasses.

- **Rent a car:** The best way to explore the Costa Smeralda is by car. This will give you the flexibility to visit all of the different villages and beaches at your own pace.

- **Be prepared for high prices:** The Costa Smeralda is a luxury destination, so prices for food, drinks, and accommodations can be high. Be sure to budget accordingly.

Costa Paradiso: Rugged Beauty

Costa Paradiso, or Paradise Coast, is a stretch of coastline in northwestern Sardinia that is known for its dramatic cliffs, secluded coves, and crystal-clear waters. It is a lesser-known destination than the Costa Smeralda, but it is no less beautiful.

Costa Paradiso is a great place to visit if you are looking for a more relaxed and authentic Sardinian experience. The coastline is dotted with small villages and hamlets, where you can find local restaurants and shops. There are also a number of hiking trails in the area that offer stunning views of the coastline.

One of the most popular things to do in Costa Paradiso is to visit the Spiaggia Li Cossi beach. This beach is known for its white sand, turquoise waters, and dramatic rock formations. It is a popular spot for swimming, sunbathing, and snorkeling.

Another popular activity in Costa Paradiso is to take a boat trip to the nearby islands of the Maddalena Archipelago. These islands are known for their pristine beaches, crystal-clear waters, and diverse marine life.

If you are looking for a more adventurous activity, you can try rock climbing or hiking in the Costa Paradiso mountains. There are a number of hiking trails in the area that offer stunning views of the coastline and the surrounding countryside.

Costa Paradiso is a great place to visit if you are looking for a coastal destination that offers rugged beauty, secluded beaches, and authentic Sardinian culture.

Tips for visiting Costa Paradiso:

- **Book your accommodations in advance:** Costa Paradiso is a popular destination, so it is important to book your accommodations well in advance, especially if you are traveling during the peak season (June-August).

- **Rent a car**: The best way to explore Costa Paradiso is by car. This will give you the flexibility to visit all of the different villages and beaches at your own pace.

- Be prepared for dirt roads: Many of the roads in Costa Paradiso are dirt roads, so be sure to drive carefully.

- **Pack for all types of weather**: The weather in Costa Paradiso can be unpredictable, so it is important to pack for all types of weather. Be sure to bring a jacket or sweater, as well as sunscreen and sunglasses.

Oristano Beaches: Tranquil Escapes

Sardinia is an island paradise known for its stunning beaches, crystal-clear waters, and rugged mountains. While the Costa Smeralda and Costa Paradiso are two of the most popular coastal destinations on the island, there are many other hidden gems to be discovered.

One such gem is the province of Oristano, which is home to some of the most beautiful and tranquil beaches on Sardinia. Here are a few of our favorites:

- Is Arenas Beach is located near the town of Torre Grande and is known for its long stretch of fine white sand and turquoise waters. The beach is also home to a number of sea turtles, making it a great place for snorkeling and diving.

- Cala Sa Conca Beach is a secluded beach located near the town of Cabras. The beach is surrounded by pine trees and juniper bushes, making it a great place to relax and escape the crowds.

- San Giovanni di Sinis Beach is a long stretch of sandy beach located near the town of Tharros. The beach is popular with windsurfers and kitesurfers, but there are also plenty of secluded spots where you can relax and enjoy the peace and quiet.

- Torre Grande Marina is a small marina located in the town of Torre Grande. The marina is surrounded by a number of restaurants and bars, making it a great place to enjoy a meal or drink while watching the sunset.

- Spiaggia di Mari Ermi Beach is a long stretch of sandy beach located near the town of Arborea. The beach is popular with families, as it is shallow and has calm waters.

Oristano is also home to a number of other attractions, such as the ancient ruins of Tharros, the town of Cabras, and the Sinis Peninsula.

If you are looking for a coastal destination that offers stunning scenery, tranquil beaches, and authentic Sardinian culture, then the province of Oristano is the perfect place for you.

Here are a few tips for planning your trip to Oristano:

- Book your accommodations in advance: Oristano is a popular tourist destination, so it is important to book your accommodations well in advance, especially if you are traveling during the peak season (June-August).

- Rent a car: The best way to explore Oristano and its beaches is by car. This will give you the flexibility to visit all of the different beaches and attractions at your own pace.

- Be prepared for hot weather: The weather in Oristano can be very hot during the summer months, so be sure to pack sunscreen and a hat.

- Pack for all types of weather: The weather in Oristano can also be unpredictable, so be sure to pack for all types of weather, including a jacket or sweater.

Sardinia's Eastern Coast: Hidden Gems

Sardinia's eastern coast is a treasure trove of hidden gems, from secluded beaches to charming villages to ancient ruins. If you're looking for a more authentic Sardinian experience, away from the crowds of the Costa Smeralda, be sure to check out these hidden gems:

Cala Brandinchi Beach: This stunning beach is known for its white sand, turquoise waters, and towering pine trees. It's often referred to as "Little Tahiti" due to its resemblance to the South Pacific island.

Cala Luna Beach: This secluded beach is located in a cove at the end of a narrow gorge. It's a popular spot for swimming, sunbathing, and hiking.

Cala Goloritze Beach: This picturesque beach is surrounded by dramatic limestone cliffs and crystal-clear waters. It's a popular spot for snorkeling and diving.

Torre di Porto Giunco Beach: This beach is known for its white sand, turquoise waters, and iconic Spanish tower. It's a popular spot for swimming, sunbathing, and watching the sunset.

Capo Ferrato Lighthouse: This lighthouse is located on a promontory at the southern tip of Sardinia. It offers stunning views of the coastline and the surrounding islands.

Bosa Village: This picturesque village is located on the Temo River. It's known for its colorful houses, narrow streets, and medieval castle.

Alghero Village: This charming village is located on the northwestern coast of Sardinia. It's known for its Catalan heritage, medieval architecture, and sparkling beaches.

Tharros Ruins: This ancient Phoenician city was founded in the 8th century BC. It's home to a number of well-preserved ruins, including a temple, theater, and necropolis.

Nuraghe Giants Tomb: This ancient burial tomb is one of the largest and best-preserved in Sardinia. It was built by the Nuraghic people, who lived on the island from around 1800 to 500 BC.

These are just a few of the many hidden gems to be discovered on Sardinia's eastern coast. With its stunning scenery, charming villages, and ancient ruins, there's something for everyone to enjoy in this beautiful region.

Here are a few tips for planning your trip:

- Book your accommodations in advance, especially if you're traveling during the peak season (June-August).

- Rent a car to give you the flexibility to explore at your own pace.

- Pack for all types of weather, as the weather in Sardinia can be unpredictable.

- Bring sunscreen, a hat, and sunglasses to protect yourself from the sun.

- Be sure to sample some of the local cuisine, such as fresh seafood, pasta dishes, and Sardinian cheese.

Inland Adventures

Barbagia Region: Heart of Sardinia

The Barbagia region is the beating heart of Sardinia, an island paradise in the Mediterranean Sea. Located in the center of the island, the Barbagia is a mountainous region with a rich history and culture.

The Barbagia region is home to a number of ancient villages, each with its own unique character. Some of the most popular villages to visit include Orgosolo, Fonni, and Mamoiada.

Orgosolo is known for its murals, which depict scenes from Sardinian history and culture. Fonni is the highest village in Sardinia and is a popular destination for hiking and skiing. Mamoiada is known for its traditional masks, which are worn during the Mamuthones festival.

In addition to its villages, the Barbagia region is also home to a number of natural attractions, including the Gennargentu Mountains, the Supramonte plateau, and the Gologone springs.

The Gennargentu Mountains are the highest mountains in Sardinia and offer stunning views of the surrounding countryside. The Supramonte plateau is a vast wilderness area with limestone cliffs, gorges, and caves. The Gologone springs are a series of natural springs located in a beautiful valley.

The Barbagia region is a great place to experience authentic Sardinian culture. The people of the Barbagia are known for their hospitality and their love of tradition.

Here are a few things you can do during your visit to the Barbagia region:

- **Visit the ancient villages**: The villages of the Barbagia region are home to a number of historical and cultural attractions. Be sure to visit the murals in Orgosolo, the traditional masks in Mamoiada, and the medieval castle in Oliena.

- **Hike in the Gennargentu Mountains**: The Gennargentu Mountains offer some of the best hiking in Sardinia. Be sure to hike to the top of Punta La Marmora, the highest peak in Sardinia.

- **Visit the Supramonte plateau**: The Supramonte plateau is a vast wilderness area with stunning scenery. Be sure to visit the

Gorropu Gorge, one of the deepest gorges in Europe.

- **Swim in the Gologone springs:** The Gologone springs are a series of natural springs located in a beautiful valley. Be sure to take a swim in the crystal-clear waters.

- **Sample the local cuisine:** The Barbagia region is known for its delicious cuisine. Be sure to try some of the local dishes, such as pane carasau (thin, crispy bread), malloreddus (gnocchi-like pasta), and pecorino sardo (sheep's milk cheese).

The Barbagia region is a truly special place, offering visitors a chance to experience the heart of Sardinia. With its stunning scenery, ancient villages, and rich culture, the Barbagia region is a must-visit for anyone traveling to Sardinia.

Here are a few tips for planning your trip to the Barbagia region:

- Book your accommodations in advance, especially if you're traveling during the peak season (June-August).

- Rent a car to give you the flexibility to explore at your own pace.

- Wear comfortable shoes, as you'll be doing a lot of walking.

- Bring sunscreen, a hat, and sunglasses to protect yourself from the sun.

- Be sure to sample some of the local cuisine, such as fresh seafood, pasta dishes, and Sardinian cheese.

Gennargentu National Park: Hiking Paradise

Gennargentu National Park is a hiker's paradise, with over 200 kilometers of marked trails winding through stunning scenery, including mountains, valleys, forests, and rivers.

The park is home to the highest peak in Sardinia, Punta La Marmora, which offers breathtaking views of the island. Other popular hiking destinations include the Gorropu Gorge, one of the deepest gorges in Europe, and the Supramonte plateau, a vast wilderness area with limestone cliffs, caves, and forests.

There are trails for all levels of hikers in Gennargentu National Park, from easy walks to challenging climbs. Some of the most popular trails include:

- **Su Gorropu Gorge**: This trail takes hikers through the deepest gorge in Europe, with stunning limestone cliffs and waterfalls. The trail is challenging, but it is well worth the effort for the incredible views.

- **Punta La Marmora**: This trail leads to the highest peak in Sardinia, offering breathtaking views of the island. The trail is moderate in difficulty, but it is important to be prepared for the altitude.

- **Sa Conca de Mannu:** This easy trail takes hikers through a beautiful forest to a natural pool, where you can take a refreshing swim.

- **Su Crastu Is Pischinas**: This trail takes hikers to a natural waterfall, where you can swim and cool off on a hot day.

- **Sedda Arba**: This moderate trail offers stunning views of the Gennargentu Mountains and the surrounding countryside.

No matter what your level of experience, you're sure to find a trail to your liking in Gennargentu National Park. Here are a few tips for planning your hike:

- Wear comfortable shoes and clothing. The trails in Gennargentu National Park can be rocky and uneven, so it is important to wear comfortable shoes and clothing.

- Bring plenty of water and snacks. There are no facilities on most of the trails in Gennargentu National Park, so it is important to bring plenty of water and snacks.

- Be aware of the weather conditions. The weather in Gennargentu National Park can change quickly, so it is important to be aware of the forecast and dress appropriately.

- Let someone know where you are going. Before you set out on your hike, be sure to let someone know where you are going and when you expect to be back.

Gennargentu National Park is a truly special place, offering visitors a chance to experience the best of Sardinia. With its stunning scenery, challenging hikes, and rich culture, Gennargentu National Park is a must-visit for any outdoor enthusiast.

Traditional Villages and Culture

Sardinia is an island in the Mediterranean Sea with a rich and unique culture. The island is home to a number of traditional villages, each with its own unique character. These villages offer visitors a chance to experience the authentic side of Sardinian culture.

Orgosolo is one of the most popular traditional villages to visit in Sardinia. The village is known for its murals, which depict scenes from Sardinian history and culture. Orgosolo is also home to a number of traditional shops and restaurants, where you can sample the local cuisine.

Fonni is another popular traditional village to visit in Sardinia. The village is located in the Gennargentu Mountains and is a popular destination for hiking and skiing. Fonni is also home to a number of traditional festivals, including the Barbagia Festival, which takes place every summer.

Mamoiada is a traditional village in the Barbagia region of Sardinia. The village is known for its Mamuthones festival, which takes place every winter. The festival features men wearing traditional masks and costumes. Mamoiada is also home to a number of traditional shops and restaurants, where you can sample the local cuisine.

Oliena is a traditional village in the Barbagia region of Sardinia. The village is known for its medieval castle, which is one of the best-preserved in Sardinia. Oliena is also home to a number of traditional festivals, including the Su Gologone festival, which takes place every summer.

Alghero is a traditional village on the northwest coast of Sardinia. The village is known for its Catalan heritage, which is evident in its architecture, language, and cuisine. Alghero is also home to a number of beautiful beaches, making it a popular destination for swimming and sunbathing.

These are just a few of the many traditional villages to visit in Sardinia. Each village has its own unique character and charm. Be sure to visit a few of these villages during your trip to Sardinia to experience the authentic side of Sardinian culture.

Other Traditional Villages in Sardinia:

- Atzara
- Bosa
- Carloforte
- Castelsardo
- Posada
- Samugheo
- Santadi
- Sorgono
- Teti

Sardinian Culture:

Sardinian culture is a blend of influences from different cultures, including the Phoenicians, Romans, Greeks, Arabs, and Spaniards. The Sardinian people are known for their hospitality, their love of tradition, and their strong sense of community.

Some of the most important aspects of Sardinian culture include:

- **Food and wine:** Sardinia is known for its delicious cuisine, which includes fresh seafood, pasta dishes, and Sardinian cheese. The island is also home to a number of award-winning wineries.

- **Music and dance:** Sardinian music and dance are an important part of the island's culture. There are a number of traditional Sardinian dances, such as the ballu tundu and the su ballu sardu.

- **Festivals**: Sardinia is home to a number of traditional festivals, which are held throughout the year. These festivals celebrate the island's culture and traditions.

Tips for Visiting Traditional Villages in Sardinia:

- Be respectful of the local culture and traditions.

- Learn a few basic Sardinian phrases.

- Dress modestly, especially when visiting religious sites.

- Support the local economy by shopping at local shops and eating at local restaurants.

- Be prepared for crowds, especially during the peak season (June-August).

Nuragic Sites: Ancient Wonders

The Nuragic people were a civilization that inhabited Sardinia from around 1800 to 500 BC. They left behind a number of impressive ruins, including nuraghi, which are tower-like structures, and giant statues.

Nuraghi are thought to have been used for a variety of purposes, including defense, storage, and religious rituals. They are typically made of stone and have a beehive-shaped dome. The largest nuraghi can be up to 20 meters tall.

The Giants of Monte Prama are a series of four giant statues that were discovered in Sardinia in 1974. The statues are carved from sandstone and are over two meters tall. They are thought to have been created by the Nuragic people in the 8th century BC.

Nuragic sites are found all over Sardinia, but some of the most popular to visit include:

- **Su Nuraxi di Barumini:** This UNESCO World Heritage Site is home to one of the best-preserved nuraghi in Sardinia.

- **Giants of Monte Prama:** This archaeological site is home to the four giant statues that were discovered in 1974.

- **Nuraghe Losa:** This nuraghe is located in a beautiful setting and offers stunning views of the surrounding countryside.

- **Nuraghe Palmavera**: This nuraghe is located near the town of Alghero and is home to a museum that houses artifacts from the Nuragic period.

Nuragic sites offer visitors a chance to learn about the ancient civilization that inhabited Sardinia. The ruins are impressive and offer a glimpse into the past. If you are interested in history and archaeology, then you should definitely visit a Nuragic site during your trip to Sardinia.

Tips for Visiting Nuragic Sites:

- Wear comfortable shoes, as you will be doing a lot of walking.

- Bring water and snacks, as there are no facilities at most of the sites.

- Be aware of the weather conditions and dress appropriately.

- Be respectful of the ruins and do not touch or damage them.

Chapter 4: Sardinian Culture and Traditions

Festivals and Celebrations

Sa Sartiglia: Carnival in Oristano

Sa Sartiglia is a traditional equestrian carousel tournament held in the town of Oristano, Sardinia, Italy, during the Carnival season. It is one of the most popular and important festivals on the island, and is known for its spectacular costumes, horsemanship, and jousting.

The festival takes place on the last Sunday and Tuesday of Carnival, and is divided into two main parts: the Giostra alla Stella (Joust of the Star) and the Pariglie.

Giostra alla Stella

The Giostra alla Stella is the main event of Sa Sartiglia, and is a jousting tournament in which riders attempt to spear a silver star suspended from a rope. The event is preceded by a parade of riders, who wear colorful costumes and masks.

The riders are divided into two teams, the Su Componidori (the Defenders) and the Su Re e sa Regina (the King and Queen). Each team has a leader, known as the Componidore or the Re (King).

The Giostra alla Stella begins with the Componidori charging at the star. If the Componidore succeeds in spearing the star, it is a good sign for the coming year. If he fails, it is a bad omen.

Pariglie

The Pariglie is a series of acrobatic horse stunts performed by the riders. The stunts are designed to show off the riders' horsemanship and skill.

The Pariglie is a less formal event than the Giostra alla Stella, and the riders are allowed to compete individually or in teams. The stunts are judged by a panel of judges, and the winner is awarded a prize.

Other Events

There are a number of other events that take place during Sa Sartiglia. These include:

- **Su Scurridore**: A race in which riders race their horses through the town streets.

- **Sa Corsa alla Quintana**: A race in which riders race their horses to the center of the town square, where they try to pick up a ring suspended from a rope.

- **Su Spingarda**: A parade of riders who fire blank bullets from their muskets.

- **Sa Remada**: A race in which riders race their horses to the sea, where they try to retrieve a coin from the water.

Tips for Attending Sa Sartiglia

- Book your accommodation in advance, especially if you are traveling during the peak season (February).

- Arrive early to get a good spot to watch the events.

- Be prepared for crowds, especially during the Giostra alla Stella.

- Be respectful of the local culture and traditions.

- Wear comfortable shoes, as you will be doing a lot of walking.

- Bring sunscreen and sunglasses, as the weather can be sunny in February.

Sa Sartiglia is a unique and unforgettable festival that offers visitors a chance to experience authentic Sardinian culture. If you are visiting Sardinia during the Carnival season, be sure to check out Sa Sartiglia. You won't be disappointed!

Traditional Sardinian Dress

Traditional Sardinian dress is a vibrant and colorful reflection of the island's rich culture and history. The costumes vary from region to region, but they all share a few common features: bold colors, intricate embroidery, and elaborate jewelry.

Women's Dress

Traditional Sardinian dress for women typically consists of a long, pleated skirt, a fitted bodice, and a shawl. The skirt is often made of a brightly colored fabric, such as wool, velvet, or silk. The bodice is usually made of a contrasting color and is often embroidered with intricate designs. The shawl is typically made of a light fabric, such as lace or linen, and is worn over the shoulders.

Men's Dress

Traditional Sardinian dress for men typically consists of a long jacket, a waistcoat, a shirt, trousers, and a hat. The jacket is usually made of a dark fabric, such as wool or velvet. The waistcoat is often made of a contrasting color and is often embroidered with intricate designs. The shirt is usually white and is worn with a tie. The trousers are usually made of a dark fabric and are often pleated. The hat is typically made of felt or straw.

Jewelry

Sardinian jewelry is an important part of traditional Sardinian dress. The most common types of jewelry worn by Sardinian women include filigree brooches, necklaces, and earrings. Filigree is a type of metalwork that involves twisting and soldering thin wires to create intricate designs. Sardinian filigree jewelry is known for its delicate craftsmanship and beautiful designs.

Traditional Sardinian Dress Today

Traditional Sardinian dress is still worn today on special occasions, such as festivals and weddings. It is also worn by performers in traditional Sardinian dances and music.

Where to See Traditional Sardinian Dress

If you are interested in seeing traditional Sardinian dress, there are a few places where you can do so:

- **At traditional Sardinian festivals**: There are a number of traditional Sardinian festivals held throughout the year. Some of the most popular festivals include Sa Sartiglia in Oristano, Su Connari in Siligo, and Is Ardia in Sedini.

- **At traditional Sardinian music and dance performances:** Traditional Sardinian music and dance performances are held all over the island. You can find information about upcoming performances at your local tourist office.

- **At museums:** Some museums in Sardinia have exhibits on traditional Sardinian dress. One of the best places to see traditional Sardinian dress is at the Museo Nazionale Archeologico Etnografico G. A. Sanna in Sassari.

Traditional Sardinian dress is a beautiful and unique reflection of the island's rich culture and history. If you have the opportunity to see traditional Sardinian dress, be sure to take it! You won't be disappointed.

Craftsmanship and Artistry

Sardinia, an island in the Mediterranean Sea, is known for its stunning natural beauty, its rich culture, and its unique crafts and artistry. The island's artisans have been creating beautiful and functional objects for centuries, using a variety of materials and techniques.

Basketry

One of the most well-known Sardinian crafts is basketry. Sardinian baskets are made from a variety of natural materials, including reeds, rushes, and willow. The baskets are typically woven using traditional techniques that have been passed down from generation to generation.

Sardinian baskets are known for their durability, their intricate designs, and their vibrant colors. They are used for a variety of purposes, including carrying food and water, storing goods, and decorating homes.

Knifemaking

Another popular Sardinian craft is knifemaking. Sardinian knives are known for their high quality and their distinctive design. The blades are typically made of high-carbon steel, and the handles are often made of wood, horn, or bone.

Sardinian knives are used for a variety of purposes, including cooking, hunting, and self-defense. They are also popular collectors' items.

Jewelry Making

Sardinian jewelry is known for its intricate designs and its use of precious metals and gemstones. Sardinian jewelers use a variety of techniques, including filigree, granulation, and enameling.

Sardinian jewelry is typically made of gold, silver, and coral. The jewelry is often decorated with intricate designs, such as flowers, animals, and geometric patterns.

Ceramics

Sardinian ceramics are known for their simple designs and their earthy colors. Sardinian potters use a variety of traditional techniques to create their work.

Sardinian ceramics are typically made of clay and are fired in wood-fired kilns. The ceramics are often decorated with simple designs, such as geometric patterns and symbols.

Wood Carving

Sardinian wood carving is a tradition that dates back centuries. Sardinian wood carvers use a variety of techniques to create their work, including carving, chiseling, and pyrography.

Sardinian wood carvings are typically made of olive wood, juniper wood, or chestnut wood. The carvings are often decorated with intricate designs, such as animals, flowers, and religious symbols.

Where to Buy Sardinian Crafts and Art

Sardinian crafts and art can be purchased at a variety of locations on the island, including:

- **Village markets**: Many villages in Sardinia have weekly markets where local artisans sell their wares.

- **Craft shops**: There are a number of craft shops located throughout Sardinia where you can purchase Sardinian crafts and art.

- **Art galleries:** There are also a number of art galleries in Sardinia that sell Sardinian crafts and art.

Tips for Buying Sardinian Crafts and Art

When buying Sardinian crafts and art, it is important to be aware of the following:

- Be prepared to bargain: Bargaining is common at village markets and craft shops.

- Ask about the materials: Be sure to ask the artisan about the materials used to make the piece you are interested in purchasing.

- Inspect the piece carefully: Be sure to inspect the piece carefully for any defects before purchasing it.

- Get a receipt: Be sure to get a receipt from the artisan, especially if you are purchasing a high-priced item.

Sardinian crafts and artistry are a reflection of the island's rich culture and heritage. If you are visiting Sardinia, be sure to take some time to browse the village markets and craft shops for unique and beautiful souvenirs. You won't be disappointed!

Sardinian Cuisine

Local Culinary Traditions

Sardinian cuisine is a unique and delicious blend of influences from the Mediterranean region. The island's cuisine is based on fresh, local ingredients, such as seafood, meat, cheese, and vegetables. Sardinian dishes are typically simple and rustic, but they are also full of flavor.

Some of the most popular Sardinian dishes include:

- Porceddu: Roasted suckling pig
- Malloreddus: Sardinian gnocchi
- Sa fregula: Sardinian couscous
- Culurgiones: Stuffed dumplings
- Pane carasau: Sardinian flatbread
- Seadas: Fried cheese pastries

Sardinian cuisine is also known for its delicious seafood dishes. Some of the most popular seafood dishes include:

- Bottarga: Salted, cured fish roe
- Sa merca: Boiled and salted mullet

- Burrida: Dogfish stew

- Arselle alla vernaccia: Clams cooked in white wine

- Fritto misto di mare: Mixed seafood fry

Sardinian cuisine is also known for its delicious cheeses. Some of the most popular Sardinian cheeses include:

- Pecorino sardo: Sheep's milk cheese

- Casu marzu: Maggot-infested sheep's milk cheese

- Ricotta sarda: Ricotta cheese

- Fiore sardo: Cow's milk cheese

- Cabra sarda: Goat's milk cheese

Sardinian cuisine is best enjoyed with a glass of local wine. Sardinia is home to a number of award-winning wineries, which produce a variety of red, white, and rosé wines.

If you are visiting Sardinia, be sure to try some of the local cuisine. You won't be disappointed!

Here are some tips for enjoying Sardinian cuisine:

- Eat at family-owned restaurants: The best way to experience Sardinian cuisine is to eat at family-owned restaurants. These restaurants typically serve traditional Sardinian dishes made with fresh, local ingredients.

- Order the daily special: Many Sardinian restaurants offer a daily special, which is typically a traditional Sardinian dish. The daily special is a great way to try a new dish and to save money.

- Don't be afraid to try new things: Sardinian cuisine has a lot to offer, so don't be afraid to try new things. Be sure to try some of the local seafood, cheeses, and wines.

- Take your time: Sardinian meals are typically leisurely affairs. So take your time and enjoy your food and company.

Here is a sample itinerary for a day of Sardinian culinary exploration:

Morning: Start your day with a breakfast of pane carasau, ricotta sarda, and coffee.

Lunch: For lunch, have a traditional Sardinian meal at a family-owned restaurant. Start with a plate of antipasti, such as olives, cheese, and cured meats. Then, order a pasta dish, such as malloreddus or culurgiones. For your main course, order a seafood dish, such as arselle alla vernaccia or fritto misto di mare. Finish your meal with a dessert, such as seadas or tiramisu.

Evening: For dinner, have a light meal at a restaurant on the beach. Start with a glass of local wine and an appetizer, such as bottarga or sa merca. Then, order a main course, such as grilled fish or seafood pasta. Finish your meal with a dessert, such as gelato or panna cotta.

MustTry Dishes and Desserts

Must-Try Dishes

Porceddu: This is the quintessential Sardinian dish: a whole suckling pig roasted over an open fire until the skin is crispy and the meat is juicy and tender. Porceddu is typically served with roasted potatoes and a simple salad.

Malloreddus: These Sardinian gnocchi are made with semolina flour and water, and are shaped like little shells. Malloreddus are typically served with a tomato sauce and sausage, but can also be served with other sauces, such as pesto or Alfredo sauce.

Sa fregula: This Sardinian couscous is made from semolina flour and water, and is roasted before being cooked. Sa fregula is typically served with seafood, but can also be served with meat or vegetables.

Culurgiones: These stuffed dumplings are made with a thin dough that is filled with a mixture of ricotta cheese, spinach, and mint. Culurgiones are typically served with a tomato sauce and grated pecorino sardo cheese.

Pane carasau: This Sardinian flatbread is made from durum wheat flour and water. It is very thin and crispy, and can be eaten on its own or used to make sandwiches or wraps.

Must-Try Desserts

Seadas: These fried cheese pastries are made with a ricotta cheese filling that is sweetened with honey and sugar. Seadas are typically served drizzled with honey and dusted with powdered sugar.

Pardulas: These small, sweet pies are made with a ricotta cheese filling that is flavored with lemon zest, saffron, and orange flower water. Pardulas are typically decorated with a lattice pattern on top.

Pabassinos: These almond cookies are made with ground almonds, sugar, and eggs. Pabassinos are typically shaped into small balls and then baked.

Tiliccas: These honey cookies are made with flour, sugar, honey, and eggs. Tiliccas are typically shaped into small cakes and then decorated with almonds or hazelnuts.

Sebadas: These cheese pastries are made with a ricotta cheese filling that is sweetened with honey and sugar. Sebadas are typically fried and then drizzled with honey.

Where to Find the Best Sardinian Food

The best Sardinian food can be found at family-owned restaurants in small villages and towns. Look for restaurants that have a daily specials menu, as this is a good sign that they are using fresh, local ingredients.

If you are looking for a more upscale dining experience, there are also a number of Sardinian restaurants in the larger cities that serve excellent food. However, it is important to book your table in advance, especially during the peak season.

Tips for Ordering Sardinian Food

- Don't be afraid to try new things: Sardinian cuisine has a lot to offer, so don't be afraid to try new things. Be sure to try some of the local seafood, cheeses, and wines.

- Take your time: Sardinian meals are typically leisurely affairs. So take your time and enjoy your food and company.

- Be prepared to pay in cash: Many Sardinian restaurants do not accept credit cards, so be sure to have some cash on hand.

Sardinian cuisine is a delicious and unique blend of influences from the Mediterranean region. The island's cuisine is based on fresh, local ingredients, such as seafood, meat, cheese, and vegetables. Sardinian dishes are typically simple and rustic, but they are also full of flavor.

If you are visiting Sardinia, be sure to try some of the local cuisine. You won't be disappointed!

Wines and Liquors

Sardinia is also known for its excellent wines and liquors. The island is home to a number of award-winning wineries, which produce a variety of red, white, and rosé wines. Some of the most popular Sardinian wines include:

Cannonau di Sardegna: This red wine is made from the Cannonau grape, which is a native Sardinian grape. Cannonau di Sardegna is typically full-bodied and has flavors of black fruit, spice, and herbs.

Vermentino di Sardegna: This white wine is made from the Vermentino grape, which is also a native Sardinian grape. Vermentino di Sardegna is typically light-bodied and has flavors of citrus fruit, white flowers, and almonds.

Nasco di Cagliari: This sweet wine is made from the Nasco grape, which is a native Sardinian grape. Nasco di Cagliari is typically full-bodied and has flavors of honey, dried fruit, and nuts.

Sardinia is also home to a number of traditional liquors, including:

Mirto: This liqueur is made from the myrtle berry, which is a native Sardinian plant. Mirto is typically sweet and has a strong flavor of myrtle berry.

Filu ferru: This grappa is made from the Cannonau grape. Filu ferru is typically clear and has a strong flavor of grape.

Acquavite: This brandy is made from the Cannonau grape and is typically aged in oak barrels. Acquavite is typically amber in color and has a complex flavor of fruit, spice, and wood.

If you are visiting Sardinia, be sure to try some of the local wines and liquors. You won't be disappointed!

Tips for Choosing and Enjoying Sardinian Wines and Liquors

When choosing Sardinian wines, it is important to consider the following factors:

- **The grape variety:** Sardinia is home to a number of unique grape varieties, such as Cannonau, Vermentino, and Nasco. Be sure to try some of the local grape varieties to get a taste of Sardinia's unique terroir.

- **The region of production**: Sardinia is divided into a number of different wine regions, each with its own unique characteristics. Be sure to try wines from different regions to get a sense of the diversity of Sardinian wine.

- **The price**: Sardinian wines range in price from affordable to expensive. Be sure to set a budget before you start shopping.

When enjoying Sardinian wines and liquors, it is important to consider the following tips:

- **Serve wines at the correct temperature:** Red wines should be served at room temperature, while white wines should be served chilled.

- **Pair wines with food**: Sardinian wines pair well with a variety of foods, including seafood, pasta, and cheese. Be sure to experiment to find your favorite pairings.

- **Enjoy liquors responsibly:** Sardinian liquors are typically high in alcohol content, so be sure to enjoy them responsibly.

Dining Etiquette

Sardinian dining etiquette is a reflection of the island's rich culture and traditions. Sardinians are known for their hospitality and their love of food, and they take great pride in their cuisine. If you are invited to a Sardinian home for dinner, be sure to follow these dining etiquette tips to ensure a pleasant and enjoyable experience.

Before the Meal

- **Arrive on time:** Sardinians are punctual people, so it is important to arrive on time for your meal. If you are running late, be sure to call your host ahead of time to let them know.

- **Bring a gift:** It is customary to bring a small gift for your host when you are invited to a Sardinian home for dinner. A bottle of wine, a box of chocolates, or a bouquet of flowers are all appropriate gifts.

- **Dress appropriately:** Sardinians typically dress casually for dinner. However, it is important to avoid dressing too casually, especially if you are visiting a formal household.

At the Table

- **Wait to be seated:** Your host will typically show you to your seat at the table.

- **Use your utensils correctly**: Sardinians use the continental style of eating, which means that they hold their fork in their left hand and their knife in their right hand.

- **Pace yourself**: Sardinian meals typically consist of several courses, so it is important to pace yourself. Don't feel like you have to finish everything on your plate.

- **Don't be afraid to try new things:** Sardinian cuisine is known for its unique and delicious dishes. Be sure to try some of the local dishes, even if they are not familiar to you.

During the Meal

- Enjoy your food: Sardinians take great pride in their cuisine, so be sure to enjoy your food. Let your host know how much you are enjoying the meal by complimenting them on the food.

- Engage in conversation: Sardinians are known for their hospitality and their love of conversation. Be sure to engage in conversation with your host and other guests at the table.

- Don't talk about business: It is generally considered taboo to talk about business at the dinner table in Sardinia. Instead, focus on light and pleasant conversation.

After the Meal

- Thank your host: Be sure to thank your host for the delicious meal and for their hospitality.

- Help to clean up: It is customary to help to clean up after dinner in Sardinia. Offer to help your host with the dishes or to put away the food.

- Leave a tip: It is not customary to leave a tip at restaurants in Sardinia. However, you may want to leave a small tip if you are very impressed with the service.

- Don't refuse food: It is considered rude to refuse food when you are invited to a Sardinian home for dinner. If you are not hungry, you can always ask for a smaller portion or save the food for later.

- Don't get drunk: It is considered rude to get drunk at the dinner table in Sardinia. Drink in moderation and enjoy your meal.

- Don't leave early: It is considered rude to leave early from a Sardinian dinner party.

Wait until the other guests have left before you say goodbye to your host.

By following these dining etiquette tips, you can ensure a pleasant and enjoyable dining experience in Sardinia. Sardinians are very welcoming and hospitable people, and they will appreciate your efforts to follow their customs and traditions.

Chapter 5: MustSee Cities and Towns

Cagliari: The Capital

Historic Districts and Landmarks

Cagliari, the capital of Sardinia, is a city with a rich history dating back over 2,000 years. The city is home to a number of historic districts and landmarks, which are well worth a visit.

Castello

The Castello district is the oldest part of Cagliari and is located on a hill overlooking the city. The district is home to a number of historic buildings, including the Cagliari Cathedral, the Palazzo Regio (Royal Palace), and the Elephant Tower.

The Cagliari Cathedral is a Romanesque cathedral that was built in the 13th century. The cathedral is known for its beautiful facade and its interior, which is decorated with frescoes and mosaics.

The Palazzo Regio is a former royal palace that was built in the 14th century. The palace is now a museum that houses a collection of Sardinian art and artifacts.

The Elephant Tower is a 14th-century tower that was built to protect the city from invaders. The tower is located on the highest point in the Castello district and offers stunning views of the city and the surrounding area.

Stampace

The Stampace district is a lively and colorful district that is located at the foot of the Castello hill. The district is known for its narrow streets, its lively markets, and its traditional Sardinian restaurants.

Marina

The Marina district is a modern district that is located along the Cagliari waterfront. The district is home to a number of marinas, restaurants, and shops.

Other Landmarks

Other notable landmarks in Cagliari include:

- The National Archaeological Museum, which houses a collection of artifacts from Sardinia's ancient past.

- The Roman Amphitheater, which was built in the 2nd century AD and could seat up to 10,000 spectators.

- The Basilica of San Saturnino, a Romanesque basilica that was built in the 5th century AD.

- The Santuario di Bonaria, a 14th-century church that is home to a statue of the Virgin Mary that is said to be miraculous.

Tips for Visiting Cagliari's Historic Districts and Landmarks

- Wear comfortable shoes, as you will be doing a lot of walking.

- Bring water and snacks, as there are not always places to buy food and drinks in the historic districts.

- Be respectful of the local culture and traditions.

- Be aware of your surroundings and take precautions to avoid pickpocketing and other crimes.

Local Culture and Cuisine

Cagliari, the capital of Sardinia, is a city with a rich culture and cuisine that is influenced by its Mediterranean location and its long history.

Culture

The people of Cagliari are known for their hospitality and their love of life. They are also proud of their Sardinian heritage and culture.

One of the most important aspects of Sardinian culture is family. Families are typically very close and spend a lot of time together. Another important aspect of Sardinian culture is food. Sardinians love to eat and they take great pride in their cuisine.

Some of the most popular cultural events in Cagliari include:

Sa Sartiglia: A traditional jousting tournament that is held in the town of Oristano, about an hour north of Cagliari.

Su Connari: A traditional Sardinian dance festival that is held in the town of Siligo, about 45 minutes north of Cagliari.

Is Ardia: A traditional Sardinian horse race that is held in the town of Sedini, about an hour and a half north of Cagliari.

Cuisine

Sardinian cuisine is known for its fresh, local ingredients and its simple but flavorful dishes. Some of the most popular Sardinian dishes include:

- Porceddu: Roasted suckling pig
- Malloreddus: Sardinian gnocchi
- Sa fregula: Sardinian couscous
- Culurgiones: Stuffed dumplings
- Pane carasau: Sardinian flatbread

Sardinian cuisine is also known for its excellent wines and liquors. Some of the most popular Sardinian wines include:

- Cannonau di Sardegna: A full-bodied red wine

- Vermentino di Sardegna: A light-bodied white wine

- Nasco di Cagliari: A sweet wine

Some of the most popular Sardinian liquors include:

- Mirto: A liqueur made from the myrtle berry

- Filu ferru: A grappa made from the Cannonau grape

- Acquavite: A brandy made from the Cannonau grape

Where to Experience Sardinian Culture and Cuisine in Cagliari

There are many places to experience Sardinian culture and cuisine in Cagliari. Here are a few suggestions:

Visit the Castello district: The Castello district is the oldest part of Cagliari and is home to a number of historic buildings, including the Cagliari Cathedral, the Palazzo Regio (Royal Palace), and the Elephant Tower. The district is also home to a number of traditional Sardinian restaurants and shops.

Visit the Stampace district: The Stampace district is a lively and colorful district that is known for its narrow streets, its lively markets, and its traditional Sardinian restaurants.

Visit the Marina district: The Marina district is a modern district that is located along the Cagliari waterfront. The district is home to a number of marinas, restaurants, and shops.

Take a cooking class: There are a number of cooking schools in Cagliari that offer classes on Sardinian cuisine. This is a great way to learn how to make some of your favorite Sardinian dishes.

Visit a winery: There are a number of wineries in the Cagliari area that offer tours and tastings. This is a great way to learn about Sardinian wine and to sample some of the local wines.

Day Trips from Cagliari

Nora

Nora is an ancient Phoenician city that is located about 40 minutes southwest of Cagliari. The city was founded in the 8th century BC and was once a major trading center. Today, Nora is a popular tourist destination due to its well-preserved ruins, which include a Roman amphitheater, a temple to Tanit, and a necropolis.

Su Nuraxi di Barumini

Su Nuraxi di Barumini is a UNESCO World Heritage Site that is located about an hour and a half north of Cagliari. The site is home to a nuraghe, which is a type of megalithic tower that was built by the Nuraghic people in the 2nd millennium BC. Su Nuraxi di Barumini is one of the best-preserved nuraghi in Sardinia and is a must-see for anyone interested in the island's history.

Grotta di Nettuno

Grotta di Nettuno is a sea cave that is located about an hour and a half northwest of Cagliari. The cave is accessible by boat or by a long staircase that descends down the cliff face. Grotta di Nettuno is known for its stunning stalagmites and stalactites, as well as its crystal-clear waters.

Carloforte

Carloforte is a town that is located on the island of San Pietro, about an hour by ferry from Cagliari. The town was founded in the 18th century by a group of Ligurian fishermen and is known for its Genoese-style architecture and its delicious seafood dishes.

Oristano

Oristano is a city that is located about an hour north of Cagliari. The city is known for its well-preserved medieval architecture, its lively markets, and its annual Sa Sartiglia jousting tournament.

Other day trip ideas from Cagliari include:

- Tharros: An ancient Phoenician city that is located about an hour and a half southwest of Cagliari.

- Bosa: A picturesque town that is located on the Temo River, about an hour and a half northeast of Cagliari.

- Alghero: A Catalan-speaking city that is located on the northwest coast of Sardinia, about two hours from Cagliari.

- Castelsardo: A medieval hilltop village that is located on the northwest coast of Sardinia, about two hours from Cagliari.

Alghero: Catalan Influence

Alghero's Old Town

Alghero is a city on the northwestern coast of Sardinia, Italy. It is known for its Catalan influence, which is evident in its architecture, language, and culture. The city's old town is particularly charming, with its narrow streets, medieval buildings, and Catalan-style balconies.

History

Alghero was founded in the 14th century by the Catalan-Aragonese. The city remained under Catalan rule for over 400 years, and this is reflected in its architecture and culture.

Language

Alghero is one of the few places in the world where Catalan is still spoken. The city's dialect of Catalan is known as Algherese and is unique to Alghero.

Culture

Alghero's Catalan heritage is evident in many aspects of its culture. For example, the city's traditional cuisine is influenced by Catalan cuisine, and many of the city's festivals and events have a Catalan flavor.

The Old Town

The old town of Alghero is the heart of the city. It is a maze of narrow streets and medieval buildings, with Catalan-style balconies and wrought-iron gates.

The old town is home to a number of important landmarks, including the Alghero Cathedral, the Church of San Francesco, and the Tower of San Giacomo.

The old town is also a great place to shop and eat. There are a number of boutiques, art galleries, and restaurants located in the narrow streets.

Things to See and Do

Here are a few things to see and do in the old town of Alghero:

- **Visit the Alghero Cathedral:** The Alghero Cathedral is a beautiful Catalan Gothic cathedral that was built in the 14th century. The cathedral is known for its stunning facade and its interior, which is decorated with frescoes and mosaics.

- **Visit the Church of San Francesco:** The Church of San Francesco is a 14th-century church that is known for its Gothic architecture and its beautiful cloister.

- **Visit the Tower of San Giacomo:** The Tower of San Giacomo is a 14th-century tower that offers stunning views of the city and the surrounding area.

- **Take a walk through the narrow streets:** The narrow streets of the old town are a great place to wander around and soak up the atmosphere. Be sure to keep an eye out for the Catalan-style balconies and wrought-iron gates.

- **Do some shopping**: There are a number of boutiques and art galleries located in the narrow streets of the old town.

- **Enjoy a meal at one of the many restaurants:** The old town is home to a number of restaurants that serve both traditional Sardinian cuisine and Catalan-inspired dishes.

Tips for Visiting the Old Town of Alghero

Here are a few tips for visiting the old town of Alghero:

- Wear comfortable shoes: The old town is a maze of narrow streets, so it is important to wear comfortable shoes.

- Bring water: The old town can get quite hot in the summer, so it is important to bring water with you.

- Be aware of your surroundings: The old town is a popular tourist destination, so it is important to be aware of your surroundings and to take precautions to avoid pickpocketing.

- Respect the local culture and traditions: The old town is a historic area, so it is important to respect the local culture and traditions.

Beaches and Waterfront

Alghero is known for its beautiful beaches and waterfront. The city has a long stretch of coastline, with a variety of beaches to choose from, including sandy beaches, rocky beaches, and secluded coves.

One of the most popular beaches in Alghero is Spiaggia di Maria Pia. This long, sandy beach is located just north of the city center and is easily accessible by bus or car. Spiaggia di Maria Pia is a great place to swim, sunbathe, and play in the sand.

Another popular beach in Alghero is Spiaggia del Lido di San Giovanni. This beach is located right in the city center and is a great place to go for a swim or a stroll along the waterfront. Spiaggia del Lido di San Giovanni is also home to a number of restaurants and bars, making it a great place to relax and enjoy a meal or a drink with friends.

If you are looking for a more secluded beach, head to Spiaggia di Le Bombarde. This beach is located about 10 kilometers north of Alghero and can be reached by car or bus. Spiaggia di Le Bombarde is a beautiful beach with white sand and crystal-clear water. It is a great place to swim, snorkel, and dive.

The Alghero waterfront is a great place to take a walk, enjoy a meal, or simply relax and people-watch. The waterfront is lined with restaurants, bars, and shops. There are also a number of benches and benches where you can sit and relax.

Here are a few tips for enjoying the beaches and waterfront of Alghero:

- **Wear sunscreen:** The sun can be very strong in Alghero, so it is important to wear sunscreen.

- **Drink plenty of water**: It is important to stay hydrated, especially on hot days.

- **Be aware of the rip currents**: Some of the beaches in Alghero have rip currents, so it is important to be aware of them and to swim in safe areas.

- **Respect the environment**: Please take your trash with you and leave the beach as you found it.

Nuraghe Palmavera

Nuraghe Palmavera is one of the most important and well-preserved nuraghi in Sardinia. It is located just outside the city of Alghero, on a hilltop overlooking the Mediterranean Sea.

Nuraghe Palmavera is a complex of nuraghic buildings, including a central tower, a village, and a necropolis. The central tower is the largest nuraghic tower in Sardinia and is over 15 meters tall. The village is made up of a number of circular huts that were used as homes. The necropolis is a burial ground that contains a number of tombs.

Nuraghe Palmavera was built in the 14th century BC by the Nuraghic people. The Nuraghic people were a mysterious civilization that lived in Sardinia from the 18th century BC to the 2nd century AD. The Nuraghic people were skilled builders and constructed a number of nuraghi throughout Sardinia.

Nuraghe Palmavera is a UNESCO World Heritage Site and is one of the most popular tourist attractions in Sardinia. Visitors to Nuraghe Palmavera can explore the central tower, the village, and the necropolis. There is also a museum on-site that houses a collection of artifacts from the Nuraghic period.

Why you should visit Nuraghe Palmavera

There are a number of reasons why you should visit Nuraghe Palmavera:

- It is one of the most important and well-preserved nuraghi in Sardinia.

- It is a UNESCO World Heritage Site.

- It offers stunning views of the Mediterranean Sea.

- It is a great place to learn about the Nuraghic people and their culture.

Tips for visiting Nuraghe Palmavera

Here are a few tips for visiting Nuraghe Palmavera:

- **Wear comfortable shoes**: The nuraghe is located on a hilltop, so it is important to wear comfortable shoes.

- **Bring water:** There are no vending machines or restaurants on-site, so it is important to bring water with you.

- **Be aware of the heat**: Sardinia can be very hot in the summer, so it is important to be aware of the heat and to take precautions to avoid heat exhaustion.

- **Take your time**: There is a lot to see and do at Nuraghe Palmavera, so take your time and enjoy the experience.

Olbia: Gateway to Costa Smeralda

Introduction to Olbia

Olbia is a city on the northeastern coast of Sardinia, Italy. It is the fifth largest city on the island and is known as the gateway to the Costa Smeralda, a world-renowned tourist destination.

Olbia is a popular destination for both Italian and international tourists. The city is home to a number of beautiful beaches, as well as a historic center with a lively atmosphere.

Here is a guide on how to navigate Olbia as a first-time traveler:

Getting to Olbia

Olbia is served by Olbia Costa Smeralda Airport (OLB), which is located just outside of the city center. The airport is well-connected to major European cities and is a popular destination for charter flights.

There are a number of ways to get from the airport to the city center, including taxi, bus, and car rental. Taxis are the most expensive option, but they are also the most convenient. Buses are more affordable, but they can be crowded and may not be direct to your destination. Car rental is a good option if you want to explore the area at your own pace.

Getting around Olbia

Olbia is a relatively small city and is easy to get around on foot. However, there is also a public bus system that connects the city center to the surrounding neighborhoods.

If you are staying in the city center, you can easily walk to most of the major attractions. However, if you are staying in one of the outlying neighborhoods, you may need to take the bus to get to the city center.

Things to do in Olbia

There are a number of things to do in Olbia, including:

Visit the historic center: The historic center of Olbia is a lively area with narrow streets, shops, and restaurants. Be sure to visit the San Simplicio Church, which is a Romanesque church that dates back to the 12th century.

Visit the Olbia Archaeological Museum: The Olbia Archaeological Museum houses a collection of artifacts from Sardinia's ancient past.

Visit the Costa Smeralda: The Costa Smeralda is a world-renowned tourist destination that is located just north of Olbia. The Costa Smeralda is known for its beautiful beaches, crystal-clear water, and luxurious resorts.

Tips for first-time travelers to Olbia

Here are a few tips for first-time travelers to Olbia:

- Learn a few basic Italian phrases: This will help you communicate with locals and get around more easily.

- Be prepared for the heat: Sardinia can be very hot in the summer, so be sure to pack light clothing and drink plenty of water.

- Be aware of your surroundings: Olbia is a relatively safe city, but it is important to be aware of pickpockets and other petty theft.

- Enjoy the food: Sardinia is known for its delicious cuisine. Be sure to try some of the local dishes, such as porceddu (roasted suckling pig), malloreddus (Sardinian gnocchi), and sa fregula (Sardinian couscous).

Luxury Resorts

Olbia is the gateway to the Costa Smeralda, Sardinia's most exclusive and glamorous resort destination. The Costa Smeralda is home to some of the most luxurious resorts in the world, where celebrities and the wealthy come to relax and enjoy the island's stunning natural beauty.

Here are a few of the most luxurious resorts in Olbia and the Costa Smeralda:

Hotel Cala di Volpe: This five-star hotel is located on the Costa Smeralda and is known for its luxurious accommodations, stunning views, and world-class service. The hotel has a private beach, a spa, and multiple restaurants.

Hotel Porto Cervo: This five-star hotel is located in the heart of the Costa Smeralda and is known for its stylish accommodations, vibrant atmosphere, and excellent service. The hotel has a private beach, a spa, and multiple restaurants.

Hotel Pitrizza: This five-star hotel is located on the Costa Smeralda and is known for its secluded setting, luxurious accommodations, and impeccable service. The hotel has a private beach, a spa, and multiple restaurants.

Hotel Il Gabbiano: This five-star hotel is located on the Costa Smeralda and is known for its intimate setting, elegant accommodations, and personalized service. The hotel has a private beach, a spa, and a restaurant.

Hotel Cala Granu: This five-star hotel is located on the Costa Smeralda and is known for its family-friendly atmosphere, spacious accommodations, and excellent service. The hotel has a private beach, a spa, and multiple restaurants.

These are just a few of the many luxurious resorts available in Olbia and the Costa Smeralda. Whether you're looking for a secluded getaway, a vibrant atmosphere, or a family-friendly resort, you're sure to find the perfect place to relax and enjoy all that this stunning island has to offer.

Tips for booking a luxury resort in Olbia and the Costa Smeralda

Here are a few tips for booking a luxury resort in Olbia and the Costa Smeralda:

- **Book early**: The best resorts in Olbia and the Costa Smeralda book up quickly, especially during the summer months. It's important to book your stay well in advance to ensure that you get the room and dates you want.

- **Compare prices:** There are a number of different websites and travel agents that offer discounts on luxury resorts. It's important to compare prices before you book to make sure that you're getting the best deal possible.

- **Read reviews:** Before you book a resort, be sure to read reviews from other guests. This will help you get a sense of the resort's atmosphere, accommodations, and amenities.

- **Consider your needs:** When choosing a resort, be sure to consider your needs. If you're traveling with children, you'll want to choose a resort that has family-friendly amenities. If you're looking for a secluded getaway, you'll want to choose a resort that is located in a quiet area.

Beaches, Dining, and Nightlife

Beaches

Olbia is home to some of the most beautiful beaches in Sardinia. Here are a few of the most popular beaches in Olbia:

- **Pittulongu Beach**: This long, sandy beach is located just north of Olbia and is known for its clear water and stunning views.

- **Bados Beach**: This popular beach is located in the heart of Olbia and is known for its lively atmosphere and variety of amenities.

- **Li Cuncheddi Beach**: This secluded beach is located south of Olbia and is known for its white sand and crystal-clear water.

- **Cala Brandinchi Beach:** This beautiful beach is located on the Costa Smeralda and is known for its pink sand and turquoise water.

- **Cala di Volpe Beach**: This exclusive beach is located on the Costa Smeralda and is known for its crystal-clear water and luxurious atmosphere.

Dining

Olbia has a vibrant dining scene, with a wide variety of restaurants to choose from. Here are a few of the most popular restaurants in Olbia:

- **Il Cavatappi**: This Michelin-starred restaurant is known for its creative and innovative cuisine.

- **Trattoria Lillicu**: This traditional Sardinian restaurant is known for its fresh seafood and pasta dishes.

- **Ristorante La Vecchia Marina**: This restaurant is located in the heart of Olbia's historic center and is known for its romantic atmosphere and delicious seafood dishes.

- **Pizzeria Il Gambero**: This popular pizzeria is known for its wood-fired pizzas and fresh ingredients.

- **Gelateria Il Pozzo:** This ice cream shop is known for its delicious homemade ice cream and gelatos.

Nightlife

Olbia has a lively nightlife scene, with a variety of bars and clubs to choose from. Here are a few of the most popular bars and clubs in Olbia:

- **Phi Beach**: This exclusive beach club is known for its world-class DJs and glamorous atmosphere.

- **Ritual Club**: This popular club is known for its electronic music and lively atmosphere.

- **Cotton Club**: This jazz club is known for its intimate setting and live music performances.

- **Kandarik**: This cocktail bar is known for its creative cocktails and lively atmosphere.

- **La Terrazza Rosa**: This rooftop bar is known for its stunning views of the city and its selection of cocktails and wines.

Excursions and Boat Tours

Excursions and Boat Tours

Olbia is a popular destination for excursions and boat tours. There are a number of different companies that offer a variety of different tours, so you're sure to find one that's perfect for you.

Here are a few of the most popular excursions and boat tours from Olbia:

Costa Smeralda Boat Tour: This tour takes you to some of the most beautiful beaches on the Costa Smeralda, including Cala Mariolu, Cala Sisine, and Cala Brandinchi.

La Maddalena Archipelago Boat Tour: This tour takes you to the La Maddalena Archipelago, a group of islands off the coast of Sardinia that are known for their stunning natural beauty.

Dolphin Watching Tour: This tour takes you out into the Mediterranean Sea in search of dolphins.

Snorkeling and Diving Tour: This tour takes you to some of the best snorkeling and diving spots in the area, where you can see a variety of marine life.

Nuraghe Palmavera Tour: This tour takes you to the Nuraghe Palmavera, a UNESCO World Heritage Site that is one of the best-preserved nuraghi in Sardinia.

Tips for booking excursions and boat tours from Olbia

Here are a few tips for booking excursions and boat tours from Olbia:

- **Book early:** The most popular excursions and boat tours fill up quickly, especially during the summer months. It's important to book your tour well in advance to ensure that you get the spot you want.

- **Compare prices:** There are a number of different companies that offer excursions and boat tours, so it's important to compare prices before you book.

- **Read reviews:** Before you book a tour, be sure to read reviews from other guests. This will help you get a sense of the tour's quality, itinerary, and guides.

- **Consider your needs**: When choosing a tour, be sure to consider your needs. If you're on a tight budget, you may want to choose a less expensive tour. If you're looking for a more personalized experience, you may want to choose a private tour.

Chapter 6: Natural Paradise

Water Sports and Activities

Sardinia, an island jewel in the Mediterranean Sea, is a paradise for water sports enthusiasts. With its crystal-clear turquoise waters, pristine beaches, and diverse marine life, Sardinia offers a world of opportunities for both adrenaline-pumping activities and leisurely pursuits. Whether you're a seasoned adventurer or a curious beginner, there's something for everyone in this aquatic wonderland.

Surfing and Windsurfing

Sardinia's coastline boasts an array of world-class surf spots, catering to surfers of all levels. The island's consistent winds and diverse waves, ranging from gentle rollers to exhilarating breaks, make it a surfer's dream destination. Popular surf spots include Porto Pollo, known for its consistent thermal winds, and Isola dei Cavoli, a renowned spot for both beginners and experts.

Kiteboarding and Stand-Up Paddleboarding

Kiteboarding and stand-up paddleboarding (SUP) are gaining popularity in Sardinia due to their accessibility and versatility. Kiteboarding combines the thrill of surfing with the power of windsurfing, while SUP offers a serene and relaxing way to explore the coastline. Popular kiteboarding spots include Cala Marina, known for its shallow waters and consistent winds, and Cala Brandinchi, a picturesque spot with a laid-back atmosphere. SUP enthusiasts can enjoy leisurely paddles along the tranquil waters of the Costa Smeralda, or venture into the marine reserves to discover hidden coves and secluded beaches.

Kayaking and Canoeing

Sardinia's calm and sheltered coves, lagoons, and rivers provide an ideal setting for kayaking and canoeing. Kayakers and canoeists can glide through the mangroves of the Orri lagoon, explore the hidden coves of the Golfo di Orosei, or paddle along the tranquil waters of the Rio Posada.

Snorkeling and Diving

Sardinia's underwater world is a treasure trove of marine life, making it a haven for snorkelers and scuba divers. The island's crystal-clear waters provide excellent visibility, allowing divers to explore the depths of the Mediterranean Sea and encounter a diverse array of marine creatures, from colorful fish and playful dolphins to majestic sea turtles and elusive sharks. Popular snorkeling and diving spots include the La Maddalena Archipelago, a protected marine park with a rich biodiversity, and the Isola Tavolara, known for its underwater caves and shipwrecks.

Sailing and Boat Tours

Sailing enthusiasts can embark on exhilarating sailing adventures along Sardinia's picturesque coastline. Experienced sailors can charter a sailboat and explore the island's hidden coves and secluded beaches, while those seeking a more relaxed experience can opt for a guided boat tour. Boat tours offer opportunities to admire the island's stunning coastal scenery, spot marine life, and enjoy the refreshing Mediterranean breeze.

Tips for Choosing Water Sports and Activities in Sardinia

- **Consider your skill level and experience:** Choose activities that match your fitness level and expertise to ensure a safe and enjoyable experience.

- **Choose the right time of year:** Sardinia's water sports season generally runs from spring to autumn, with the best conditions for surfing, kiteboarding, and windsurfing typically occurring during the summer months.

- **Research local regulations and restrictions:** Be aware of any local regulations or restrictions related to water sports activities, such as permits or designated areas.

- **Seek guidance from experienced professionals:** Consider hiring a qualified instructor or guide for activities like diving or snorkeling to ensure safety and maximize your experience.

- **Respect the marine environment:** Practice responsible behavior while enjoying water sports to protect the delicate marine ecosystem.

Sardinia's natural beauty and diverse watersports offerings make it a paradise for adventurers and nature lovers alike. Whether you're seeking adrenaline-pumping thrills or serene moments of tranquility, Sardinia's waters offer endless possibilities for exploration and enjoyment. So grab your gear, pack your sense of adventure, and discover the wonders of Sardinia's aquatic paradise.

Beach Clubs and Relaxation

Sardinia, an island jewel in the Mediterranean Sea, is renowned for its stunning beaches, crystal-clear waters, and luxurious beach clubs. These exclusive havens offer a blend of world-class amenities, exquisite cuisine, and vibrant nightlife, providing an unforgettable escape for those seeking relaxation and rejuvenation.

Phi Beach: A Symbol of Elegance and Glamour

Perched on the shores of the Costa Smeralda, Phi Beach is a sanctuary of elegance and glamour. This renowned beach club is a favorite among celebrities and jet-setters, offering a sophisticated atmosphere and unparalleled services. From its stylish lounge areas and infinity pool to its sushi restaurant and renowned DJ sets, Phi Beach epitomizes the epitome of luxury and exclusivity.

Billionaire Club: Where Luxury Meets Exhilaration

Nestled amidst the picturesque scenery of Porto Cervo, Billionaire Club is a haven for those seeking a blend of luxury and excitement. This iconic beach club boasts a captivating atmosphere, where guests can indulge in delectable cuisine, refreshing cocktails, and exhilarating parties. Billionaire Club's reputation for hosting extravagant events and attracting a glamorous clientele has solidified its position as a premier destination for those seeking the ultimate in luxury and entertainment.

Sottovento: A Tranquil Oasis by the Sea

For those seeking a more tranquil retreat, Sottovento offers a serene oasis by the sea. Located in the picturesque Cala Brandinchi, this beach club provides a haven of relaxation and rejuvenation. Guests can unwind on comfortable sun loungers, indulge in delicious Mediterranean cuisine, and soak up the breathtaking views of the turquoise waters and white sandy beaches. Sottovento's laid-back atmosphere and emphasis on wellness make it an ideal escape for those seeking serenity and rejuvenation.

Ritual Club: A Fusion of Music and Nature

Carved into the natural rock formations of Capo Ceraso, Ritual Club offers a unique fusion of music and nature. This renowned beach club is known for its vibrant atmosphere and world-class DJs, providing an electrifying nightlife experience. Guests can dance under the stars, surrounded by the stunning scenery of the Mediterranean coast, while enjoying refreshing cocktails and delectable cuisine. Ritual Club's blend of music, nature, and entertainment creates an unforgettable experience for partygoers and music enthusiasts alike.

Tips for Choosing Beach Clubs in Sardinia

- Consider your preferences: Choose a beach club that aligns with your preferences for atmosphere, amenities, and clientele.

- Research and book in advance: Popular beach clubs tend to fill up quickly, especially during peak season, so plan your visit accordingly.

- Respect the dress code: Some beach clubs have specific dress codes, so check their guidelines beforehand.

- Embrace the experience: Allow yourself to unwind and enjoy the unique atmosphere, amenities, and services that each beach club has to offer.

Sardinia's beach clubs offer a world of possibilities for relaxation, rejuvenation, and unforgettable experiences. From the sophisticated elegance of Phi Beach to the vibrant energy of Ritual Club, there's a beach club to suit every taste and preference. Whether you seek tranquil escapes, exhilarating parties, or a blend of both, Sardinia's beach clubs provide the perfect setting to unwind, indulge, and create lasting memories.

Hiking and Trekking Adventures

Supramonte Mountains

Sardinia, an island jewel in the Mediterranean Sea, is home to a diverse landscape of mountains, forests, and coastlines. Among its natural wonders are the Supramonte Mountains, a rugged and awe-inspiring range that offers a paradise for hiking and trekking enthusiasts.

The Supramonte Mountains span the eastern part of Sardinia, stretching from the Gulf of Orosei in the north to the Gulf of Cagliari in the south. The range is characterized by its limestone karst formations, creating a unique landscape of jagged peaks, deep canyons, and hidden caves.

Hiking Trails for Every Level

The Supramonte Mountains offer a variety of hiking trails to suit all levels of experience, from leisurely strolls through scenic valleys to challenging ascents to mountain summits. Some of the most popular trails include:

- **Gola di Gorropu**: This breathtaking gorge is Europe's deepest canyon, offering dramatic views and a challenging hike through narrow passages and steep inclines.

- **Gorgo di Su Gorropu**: This natural monument is a secluded oasis within the

Supramonte Mountains, featuring a lush vegetation and a crystal-clear stream.

- **Nuraghe Sisine:** This ancient nuragic site offers a blend of history and hiking, with a trail leading to the ruins of an impressive nuraghe, a prehistoric Sardinian tower.

- **Taccu Mannu**: This hike leads to the summit of Mount Taccu Mannu, the highest peak in the Supramonte Mountains, offering panoramic views of the surrounding landscape.

- **Le Vie dei Nuraghi**: This network of trails connects several nuragic sites in the Supramonte Mountains, providing a historical and cultural immersion alongside a scenic hiking experience.

Planning Your Hiking Adventure

Before embarking on your hiking adventure in the Supramonte Mountains, it's essential to plan and prepare adequately to ensure a safe and enjoyable experience. Here are some tips:

- **Choose the right trail:** Select a trail that matches your fitness level and experience. Be mindful of the trail's length, elevation gain, and difficulty level.

- **Check weather conditions:** Check the weather forecast before heading out, as conditions can change rapidly in mountainous areas. Be prepared for rain, wind, and temperature fluctuations.

- **Pack appropriate gear**: Wear comfortable hiking shoes, bring plenty of water and snacks, and pack appropriate clothing for the weather conditions. Consider carrying a map, compass, or GPS device for navigation.

- **Inform others of your itinerary:** Let someone know your hiking plan, including the trail you intend to take and the expected time of return.

- **Respect the natural environment**: Leave no trace of your visit. Dispose of waste properly and avoid damaging vegetation or wildlife.

Safety and Precautions

Hiking in the Supramonte Mountains requires caution and adherence to safety guidelines:

- **Be aware of your surroundings**: Watch your footing on uneven terrain and be mindful of potential hazards such as loose rocks, cliffs, and hidden drops.

- **Avoid hiking alone**: Always hike with a companion or join a guided group. In case of an emergency, having someone with you can provide assistance.

- **Carry a first-aid kit:** Be prepared to handle minor injuries by carrying a first-aid kit with essential supplies.

- **Stay hydrated:** Drink plenty of water throughout your hike to stay hydrated, especially in warm weather.

- **Be aware of wildlife:** While encountering wildlife is rare, be cautious and avoid approaching or provoking any animals you encounter.

Embrace the Experience

Hiking in the Supramonte Mountains offers a unique opportunity to explore the natural beauty of Sardinia, immerse yourself in the region's cultural heritage, and experience the thrill of challenging ascents. Remember to hike responsibly, respect the environment, and savor the unforgettable moments amidst the stunning landscapes of Supramonte.

Monte Limbara: Alpine Escape

Nestled amidst the lush landscapes of northern Sardinia, Monte Limbara stands as a majestic massif, offering a captivating blend of alpine beauty and Mediterranean charm. This natural wonder, often referred to as the "Green Roof of Sardinia," is a paradise for outdoor enthusiasts, nature lovers, and those seeking a tranquil escape from the bustling coastal areas.

A Haven for Hikers and Nature Admirers

Monte Limbara's allure lies in its diverse landscape, ranging from verdant valleys and rolling hills to dramatic rock formations and panoramic vistas. Hikers can embark on a variety of trails, each offering unique perspectives of the surrounding natural beauty. The well-maintained Sentiero dell'Acqua (Water Trail) guides hikers through a lush forest, leading to a series of cascading waterfalls. For those seeking a more challenging ascent, the Cima del Limbara Trail, with its steep inclines and breathtaking views, provides a rewarding experience.

A Realm of Cultural and Historical Significance

Monte Limbara's rich history adds another layer of fascination to this region. The mountain's slopes are dotted with ancient nuraghi, mysterious stone structures built by the Nuragic civilization, offering a glimpse into Sardinia's past. The summit of Monte Limbara is home to the Basilica della Madonna delle Grazie, a 17th-century church that offers a serene atmosphere and panoramic views of the surrounding landscape.

Experiencing the Tranquility and Serenity of Nature

Monte Limbara provides a tranquil escape from the hustle and bustle of everyday life. The mountain's serene atmosphere, fresh air, and captivating scenery offer a chance to unwind, reconnect with nature, and find inner peace. Visitors can enjoy leisurely walks amidst the lush vegetation, take in the breathtaking sunsets, and stargaze under the clear night sky.

Tips for Planning Your Monte Limbara Adventure

To ensure a safe and enjoyable experience, here are some tips for planning your Monte Limbara adventure:

- **Choose the right time of year:** The best time to visit Monte Limbara is during the spring and autumn when the weather is pleasant and there are fewer crowds.

- **Wear appropriate clothing and footwear:** Wear comfortable hiking shoes, pack layers of clothing for changing weather conditions, and bring a hat and sunscreen for protection from the sun.

- **Carry plenty of water and snacks:** Staying hydrated is essential, especially during warm weather. Pack plenty of water and snacks to keep your energy levels up.

- **Be aware of your surroundings**: Watch your footing on uneven terrain, be mindful of potential hazards, and follow established trails.

- **Respect the environment:** Leave no trace of your visit. Dispose of waste properly and avoid damaging vegetation or wildlife.

Embrace the Beauty and Tranquility of Monte Limbara

Monte Limbara, with its captivating landscapes, rich history, and tranquil atmosphere, is a true gem of Sardinia. Whether you're an avid hiker, a nature enthusiast, or simply seeking a serene escape, Monte Limbara offers an unforgettable experience that will leave you rejuvenated and inspired.

Flora and Fauna

Sardinia, an island jewel in the Mediterranean Sea, is renowned not only for its stunning beaches, crystal-clear waters, and rich cultural heritage but also for its unique and diverse flora and fauna. Due to its geographical isolation and relatively untouched natural habitats, Sardinia has become a sanctuary for a variety of plant and animal species, many of which are found nowhere else in the world.

A Botanical Paradise

Sardinia's flora is a captivating blend of Mediterranean and European species, with over 6,000 plant species recorded on the island. The landscape is characterized by evergreen shrubs and trees, such as the iconic cork oak, the fragrant juniper, and the majestic holm oak. These resilient plants have adapted to the island's dry summers and mild winters, providing a vital habitat for a variety of wildlife.

Amongst the island's botanical treasures are several endemic species, found only in Sardinia. The Sardinian arbutus, with its distinctive red bark and fragrant flowers, is a symbol of the island's natural beauty. The Sardinian orchid, with its delicate blooms and intricate patterns, is a rare and precious gem of the island's flora.

A Realm of Endemic Fauna

Sardinia's fauna is equally impressive, with over 8,000 animal species recorded on the island. The island's diverse habitats, ranging from coastal wetlands to mountainous peaks, provide a home for a variety of creatures, both large and small.

One of Sardinia's most iconic animals is the mouflon, a wild sheep with distinctive curved horns that roams the island's mountains. The Sardinian deer, a smaller and more elusive species, is also found in the island's forests. The Sardinian wild boar, a formidable yet shy creature, inhabits the island's dense vegetation.

Sardinia's coastal waters are teeming with marine life, providing a haven for dolphins, whales, and a variety of fish species. The island's lagoons and wetlands are home to an abundance of birdlife, including flamingos, herons, and egrets. The skies above Sardinia are also home to a variety of bird species, including the majestic Bonelli's eagle and the colorful Eleonora's falcon.

Protecting Sardinia's Natural Treasures

Sardinia's unique flora and fauna are a precious part of the island's natural heritage. Several national parks and nature reserves have been established to protect these vulnerable species and their habitats. Visitors to Sardinia can play a vital role in conservation efforts by respecting the environment, avoiding littering, and following designated trails.

Exploring Sardinia's Natural Wonders

Sardinia offers a wealth of opportunities to explore its natural wonders and encounter its unique flora and fauna. Guided hikes and nature tours provide a chance to learn more about the island's biodiversity and observe wildlife in their natural habitats. Birdwatching enthusiasts can enjoy the thrill of spotting migratory birds in their seasonal habitats.

Whether you're an avid naturalist, a passionate photographer, or simply an admirer of nature's beauty, Sardinia's flora and fauna will captivate your senses and leave you with unforgettable memories.

Adventure Sports

Sardinia, an island jewel in the Mediterranean Sea, is a haven for adventure sports enthusiasts. With its stunning coastline, dramatic mountains, and crystal-clear waters, Sardinia offers a world of opportunities for adrenaline-pumping activities and exhilarating experiences. Whether you're a seasoned adventurer or a curious beginner, there's something for everyone in this aquatic and terrestrial wonderland.

Surfing and Windsurfing

Sardinia's coastline boasts an array of world-class surf spots, catering to surfers of all levels. The island's consistent winds and diverse waves, ranging from gentle rollers to exhilarating breaks, make it a surfer's dream destination. Popular surf spots include Porto Pollo, known for its consistent thermal winds, and Isola dei Cavoli, a picturesque spot with a laid-back atmosphere.

Kiteboarding and Stand-Up Paddleboarding (SUP)

Kiteboarding and SUP are gaining popularity in Sardinia due to their accessibility and versatility. Kiteboarding combines the thrill of surfing with the power of windsurfing, while SUP offers a serene and relaxing way to explore the coastline and calm waters. Popular kiteboarding spots include Cala Marina, known for its shallow waters and consistent winds, and Cala Brandinchi, a stunning spot with a relaxed atmosphere. SUP enthusiasts can enjoy leisurely paddles along the tranquil waters of the Costa Smeralda, or venture into the marine reserves to discover hidden coves and secluded beaches.

Kayaking and Canoeing

Sardinia's calm and sheltered coves, lagoons, and rivers provide an ideal setting for kayaking and canoeing. Kayakers and canoeists can glide through the mangroves of the Orri lagoon, explore the hidden coves of the Golfo di Orosei, or paddle along the tranquil waters of the Rio Posada.

Snorkeling and Diving

Sardinia's underwater world is a treasure trove of marine life, making it a haven for snorkelers and scuba divers. The island's crystal-clear waters provide excellent visibility, allowing divers to explore the depths of the Mediterranean Sea and encounter a diverse array of marine creatures, from colorful fish and playful dolphins to majestic sea turtles and elusive sharks. Popular snorkeling and diving spots include the La Maddalena Archipelago, a protected marine park with a rich biodiversity, and the Isola Tavolara, known for its underwater caves and shipwrecks.

Rock Climbing and Mountaineering

Sardinia's dramatic mountains offer challenging and rewarding terrain for rock climbers and mountaineers. Experienced climbers can tackle the sheer rock faces of the Supramonte Mountains, while beginners can find less challenging routes in areas like Cala Goloritze. Mountaineers can embark on multi-day treks through the mountains, taking in breathtaking views and experiencing the island's unique natural beauty.

Tips for Choosing Adventure Sports in Sardinia

Here are a few tips for choosing adventure sports in Sardinia:

- Consider your skill level and experience: Choose activities that match your fitness level and expertise to ensure a safe and enjoyable experience.

- Choose the right time of year: Sardinia's adventure sports season generally runs from spring to autumn, with the best conditions for surfing, kiteboarding, and windsurfing typically occurring during the summer months.

- Research local regulations and restrictions: Be aware of any local regulations or restrictions related to adventure sports activities, such as permits or designated areas.

- Seek guidance from experienced professionals: Consider hiring a qualified instructor or guide for activities like diving or rock climbing to ensure safety and maximize your experience.

- Respect the environment: Practice responsible behavior while enjoying adventure sports to protect the delicate natural ecosystems.

Unleash Your Inner Adventurer in Sardinia

Sardinia's natural beauty and diverse adventure sports offerings make it a paradise for thrill-seekers and nature lovers alike. Whether you're seeking adrenaline-pumping activities or serene moments of exploration, Sardinia's adventures offer endless possibilities for excitement, discovery, and unforgettable experiences. So grab your gear, pack your sense of adventure, and discover the wonders of Sardinia's adventure sports paradise.

Chapter 7: Exploring Sardinia's History

Nuragic Civilization

Nuraghe Structures

Sardinia, an island gem nestled in the heart of the Mediterranean Sea, boasts a rich and captivating history, with its earliest known inhabitants dating back to the Paleolithic era. Among the most intriguing chapters of Sardinia's past is the Nuragic civilization, an enigmatic society that flourished on the island from the Bronze Age to the Iron Age.

The Nuragic civilization, named after its most distinctive architectural legacy, the nuraghe, left an indelible mark on Sardinia's landscape and culture. These towering, megalithic structures, scattered across the island, stand as silent sentinels of a bygone era, offering glimpses into the lives of the Nuragic people.

The nuraghe, typically constructed from local limestone, were more than just dwellings; they were multifunctional complexes that served as defensive strongholds, communal centers, and places of worship. These impressive structures, with their circular towers, intricate stonework, and labyrinthine passages, continue to fascinate and intrigue archaeologists and visitors alike.

The Nuragic civilization's origins remain shrouded in mystery, with theories suggesting influences from other Mediterranean cultures. However, the Nuragic people developed a unique and vibrant society, characterized by their distinctive architecture, craftsmanship, and social organization.

The Nuragic people were skilled metalworkers, producing a variety of bronze tools, weapons, and ornaments. They were also accomplished ceramicists, creating intricately decorated pottery that reflected their cultural and artistic expressions.

Their social structure remains a subject of debate, but it is believed that they lived in tribal communities, with each nuraghe serving as the focal point of a local group. The Nuragic people engaged in agriculture, herding, and trade, establishing connections with other Mediterranean civilizations.

The Nuragic civilization's decline is equally enigmatic, with theories suggesting factors such as internal conflicts, external invasions, or environmental changes. By the Iron Age, around 500 BC, the Nuragic civilization had waned, leaving behind a legacy of awe-inspiring nuraghe and a rich cultural heritage that continues to captivate the imagination.

Exploring Sardinia's nuraghe is an essential part of understanding the island's history and culture. These remarkable structures offer a tangible link to the Nuragic civilization, providing insights into their daily lives, their architectural prowess, and their enduring influence on Sardinia's identity.

Several nuraghe sites are open to visitors, allowing them to delve into the Nuragic world. The UNESCO World Heritage Site of Su Nuraxi di Barumini, a remarkably well-preserved nuraghe complex, offers a comprehensive understanding of these structures. Other notable sites include Nuraghe Losa, Nuraghe Arrubiu, and Nuraghe Santu Antine, each with its unique architectural features and captivating stories to tell.

Visiting these nuraghe sites is not just a historical journey; it's an opportunity to connect with the spirit of Sardinia's past. As you wander through the labyrinthine passages and gaze upon the imposing towers, imagine the lives of the Nuragic people who once inhabited these spaces. Feel the weight of history beneath your feet and the echoes of a civilization that continues to shape Sardinia's identity.

Exploring Sardinia's nuraghe is a journey into a time of mystery and wonder, a chance to uncover the secrets of a civilization that left an indelible mark on the island's landscape and culture. So, embark on this historical adventure, let the nuraghe speak to you, and immerse yourself in the captivating legacy of the Nuragic civilization.

Archeological Sites

Archaeological sites are locations where evidence of past human activity has been preserved and can be studied by archaeologists. These sites can range from small, isolated artifacts to large, complex settlements. They can be found all over the world, and they can tell us a great deal about how people lived in the past.

Some of the most famous archaeological sites in the world include the pyramids of Giza in Egypt, the ruins of Pompeii in Italy, and the ancient city of Machu Picchu in Peru. These sites have been extensively studied and have yielded a wealth of information about the cultures that created them.

However, there are many other archaeological sites that are equally important, but that are less well-known. These sites can be just as valuable in terms of their potential to tell us about the past. For example, a small village site may not seem as impressive as a pyramid, but it can provide us with insights into everyday life in the past.

Archaeological sites are important for a number of reasons. They can help us to understand the past, to learn about different cultures, and to appreciate the diversity of human experience. They can also be used to educate the public about archaeology and to promote sustainable tourism.

Here are some of the most important things to remember when visiting archaeological sites:

- Be respectful of the site and its inhabitants. Do not touch or damage any artifacts, and be aware of your surroundings.

- Do not remove anything from the site. This includes artifacts, plants, or animals.

- Follow the rules and regulations of the site. This may include staying on marked trails, not climbing on structures, and not using cameras or flash photography.

- Report any vandalism or damage to the site to the authorities.

- Learn about the site before you visit. This will help you to appreciate its significance and to get the most out of your visit.

By following these simple guidelines, you can help to protect archaeological sites for future generations to enjoy.

Here are some of the most famous archaeological sites in the world:

- The Pyramids of Giza, Egypt: These iconic pyramids were built by the pharaohs Khufu, Khafre, and Menkaure over a period of about 200 years. They are the only remaining Seven Wonders of the Ancient World.

- The Ruins of Pompeii, Italy: This ancient Roman city was buried in ash and debris from the eruption of Mount Vesuvius in 79 AD. The site has been extensively excavated, and it provides a fascinating glimpse into everyday life in the Roman Empire.

- Machu Picchu, Peru: This ancient city was built by the Incas in the 15th century. It is located high in the Andes Mountains, and it is one of the most popular tourist destinations in Peru.

- The Great Wall of China: This massive wall was built over centuries to protect China from invaders. It is one of the longest man-made structures in the world.

- The Acropolis of Athens, Greece: This ancient citadel was home to many important temples and buildings, including the Parthenon. It is a UNESCO World Heritage Site.

- The Terracotta Army, China: This army of over 8,000 clay soldiers was buried with Qin Shi Huang, the first emperor of China, in 221

BC. It is one of the most remarkable archaeological discoveries in the world.

- The Colosseum, Italy: This massive amphitheater was built in Rome in the first century AD. It was the site of gladiatorial contests and public executions.

- Chichen Itza, Mexico: This ancient Mayan city was built in the 6th century AD. It is one of the largest and best-preserved Mayan cities in the world.

- Angkor Wat, Cambodia: This massive temple complex was built in the 12th century AD. It is the largest religious monument in the world.

- Stonehenge, England: This prehistoric monument was built around 3,000 BC. It is one of the most famous archaeological sites in the world.

These are just a few of the many fascinating archaeological sites that can be found around the world. By visiting these sites, we can learn about the past, appreciate the diversity of human experience, and inspire future generations to learn and care about the world around them.

Museums and Exhibitions

Museums and exhibitions are important cultural institutions that play a vital role in preserving, sharing, and interpreting our cultural heritage. They provide a platform for showcasing art, history, science, and other areas of human knowledge and creativity. Museums and exhibitions offer a unique and engaging way to learn about the world around us, and they can inspire, educate, and entertain visitors of all ages.

Museums

Museums are permanent institutions that collect, preserve, study, interpret, and exhibit objects of cultural, artistic, or historical significance. They typically have a specific focus, such as art, history, science, or natural history, and they may also have a more general collection of objects. Museums typically have a variety of exhibitions on display, both permanent and temporary. Permanent exhibitions showcase the museum's core collection, while temporary exhibitions focus on specific themes or artists.

Exhibitions

Exhibitions are displays of objects, images, or other materials that are designed to inform, educate, or entertain visitors. They can be mounted in museums, galleries, or other public spaces. Exhibitions can be temporary or permanent, and they may focus on a specific theme, artist, or period in history.

The Importance of Museums and Exhibitions

Museums and exhibitions are important for a number of reasons. They:

- Preserve and protect our cultural heritage: Museums collect and preserve objects of cultural, artistic, or historical significance. This helps to ensure that these objects are available for future generations to study and enjoy.

- Share and interpret our cultural heritage: Museums and exhibitions make our cultural heritage accessible to the public. They provide a platform for sharing knowledge and understanding about the past and present.

- Inspire, educate, and entertain: Museums and exhibitions can be a source of inspiration, education, and entertainment. They can spark curiosity, encourage critical thinking, and provide a window into different cultures and time periods.

- Promote economic development: Museums and exhibitions can attract tourists and contribute to the local economy. They can also create jobs and stimulate economic activity in the surrounding area.

Types of Museums and Exhibitions

There are many different types of museums and exhibitions, reflecting the diversity of human knowledge and creativity. Some of the most common types include:

- Art museums: These museums collect and exhibit works of art, such as paintings, sculptures, and drawings.

- **History museums:** These museums focus on the history of a particular place, people, or period in time.

- **Science museums**: These museums explore the natural world, from the smallest atoms to the largest galaxies.

- **Children's museums**: These museums are designed specifically for children, and they typically have interactive exhibits that allow children to learn through play.

- **Natural history museums**: These museums focus on the natural world, including plants, animals, and fossils.

- **Archaeological museums**: These museums focus on the material remains of past civilizations.

Tips for Visiting Museums and Exhibitions

Here are some tips for visiting museums and exhibitions:

- **Plan your visit:** Decide which museums and exhibitions you want to visit and check their opening hours and admission fees.

- **Research the exhibitions**: Read about the exhibitions on display so you can get a sense of what you'll be seeing.

- **Allow enough time**: Don't try to rush through the exhibitions. Take your time to look at the objects and read the information cards.

- **Ask questions:** If you have any questions, don't hesitate to ask a museum staff member.

- **Take pictures:** Many museums allow visitors to take pictures. However, be sure to check the museum's policy on photography.

- **Enjoy the experience**: Museums and exhibitions are a great way to learn, be inspired, and have fun. So relax, take your time, and enjoy the experience.

Museums and exhibitions are essential cultural institutions that play a vital role in preserving, sharing, and interpreting our cultural heritage. They provide a unique and engaging way to learn about the world around us, and they can inspire, educate, and entertain visitors of all ages.

Medieval and Historic Landmarks

Castles and Fortresses

Castles and fortresses, standing as enduring testaments to human ingenuity and power, have long captured our imaginations. These majestic structures, scattered across the globe, offer a glimpse into a bygone era of chivalry, warfare, and intrigue. If you're seeking an adventure that blends historical significance with breathtaking architecture, then embarking on a journey to explore castles and fortresses is a must.

Castles: Homes of Nobility and Defenders of Realms

Castles, once the strongholds of noble families and the guardians of kingdoms, offer a fascinating glimpse into the lives of medieval royalty and aristocracy. From their imposing towers and fortified walls to their opulent interiors and grand courtyards, castles transport us to a world of knights, ladies, and grand feasts.

Step through the gates of Neuschwanstein Castle in Bavaria, Germany, and let your imagination soar amidst its fairytale-like spires and enchanting interiors. Wander through the halls of Windsor Castle in England, the oldest and largest occupied castle in the world, and feel the weight of history as you walk in the footsteps of monarchs.

Fortresses: Sentinels of Empires and Guardians of Borders

Fortresses, designed as bastions of defense and symbols of military might, stand as silent sentinels, guarding strategic locations and protecting empires. Their formidable walls, deep moats, and imposing towers evoke a sense of awe and admiration for the architectural prowess of their builders.

Explore the formidable ramparts of Carcassonne in France, a medieval city fortified with a double ring of walls and towers. Ascend the steep slopes of

Masada in Israel, a mountaintop fortress where Jewish rebels defied Roman rule. Marvel at the imposing grandeur of Mehrangarh Fort in India, a majestic sandstone fortress that dominates the skyline of Jodhpur.

Planning Your Castle and Fortress Adventure

To ensure an enriching and memorable experience, consider these tips when planning your castle and fortress exploration:

- **Choose your destinations:** Carefully select the castles and fortresses that align with your interests and historical preferences. Research their unique features, architectural styles, and historical significance.

- **Plan your itinerary:** Create a schedule that allows ample time to explore each site without feeling rushed. Consider visiting during off-seasons to avoid crowds and immerse yourself in the ambiance.

- **Book tours and guided visits**: Enhance your understanding of the castles and fortresses by joining guided tours or hiring local experts. Their insights will add depth to your experience.

- **Respect the sites:** Treat the castles and fortresses with respect, observing any rules or guidelines set by the management. Preserve these historical treasures for future generations.

- **Embrace the journey**: Allow yourself to be captivated by the stories and history embedded within these structures. Imagine the lives played out within their walls and the events that shaped their existence.

Exploring castles and fortresses is not merely a sightseeing adventure; it's a journey through time, a chance to connect with the past and appreciate the enduring legacy of human civilization. As you wander through these majestic structures, let your imagination soar, and you'll discover a world of knights, princesses, battles, and triumphs, a world where history comes alive.

Ancient Churches and Cathedrals

Across the globe, amidst bustling cities and serene countrysides, stand ancient churches and cathedrals, silent guardians of faith and testaments to human artistry. These awe-inspiring structures, with their towering spires, intricate stained glass windows, and hallowed halls, have echoed with prayers, witnessed countless ceremonies, and inspired generations of believers. Embarking on a journey to explore ancient churches and cathedrals is an invitation to delve into the heart of history, to appreciate the power of faith, and to marvel at architectural masterpieces.

Step into the Sacred Halls of Ancient Churches

Within the walls of ancient churches, time seems to stand still. The air is infused with the scent of incense and the hushed whispers of prayers. As you step through the arched doorways, you are transported into a realm of serenity and reverence.

In the heart of Rome, St. Peter's Basilica, the largest church in the world, stands as a symbol of the Catholic faith. Gaze upon Michelangelo's magnificent dome, adorned with intricate mosaics, and feel the grandeur of this awe-inspiring edifice. In Istanbul, Hagia Sophia, once a grand Byzantine church and later an Ottoman mosque, now stands as a museum, its architectural beauty a testament to the harmonious blend of cultures.

Cathedrals: Reaching for the Heavens

Cathedrals, with their soaring spires and vast interiors, have long been symbols of human aspiration and the pursuit of divinity. As you approach these majestic structures, their sheer scale and grandeur take your breath away.

In Chartres, France, Chartres Cathedral, a UNESCO World Heritage Site, stands as a masterpiece of Gothic architecture. As you step inside, let the symphony of colored light from the stained glass windows wash over you. In Cologne, Germany, Cologne Cathedral, with its twin spires reaching towards the heavens, has been a landmark for centuries. Admire the intricate carvings and the breathtaking beauty of this Gothic masterpiece.

Planning Your Sacred Journey

To fully appreciate the grandeur and significance of ancient churches and cathedrals, consider these tips when planning your journey:

- **Research your destinations**: Before setting off, research the churches and cathedrals you plan to visit. Learn about their history, architectural styles, and unique features.

- **Choose the right time to visit:** Avoid peak tourist seasons to experience a more serene and contemplative atmosphere. Consider attending services or special events to immerse yourself in the spiritual ambiance.

- **Dress respectfully:** Show respect for the sacred nature of these places by dressing modestly and avoiding disruptive behavior.

- **Be mindful of photography restrictions:** Some churches and cathedrals have restrictions on photography. Check guidelines before taking pictures.

- **Seek guidance and insights**: Consider joining guided tours or hiring local experts to gain deeper insights into the history and significance of these sacred spaces.

A Journey of Spiritual Discovery and Architectural Wonder

Exploring ancient churches and cathedrals is more than just a sightseeing adventure; it's a journey of spiritual discovery and architectural wonder. As you wander through these hallowed halls, let the stories and history embedded within these structures touch your soul. You may find yourself connecting with a deeper sense of faith, appreciating the beauty of human artistry, and gaining a profound appreciation for the enduring power of belief.

Historical Towns and Villages

Scattered across the globe, nestled amidst rolling hills, picturesque coastlines, and vibrant landscapes, lie historical towns and villages, each whispering tales of a bygone era. These charming enclaves, with their cobblestone streets, timeworn architecture, and rich cultural heritage, offer a glimpse into the past, inviting travelers to embark on a journey of discovery and enchantment.

Stepping Back in Time

As you wander through the narrow lanes of these historical towns and villages, time seems to slow down. The air is filled with the scent of freshly baked bread and the gentle murmur of conversations. You can almost hear the echoes of footsteps from centuries past, and the weight of history hangs in the air.

In the heart of Tuscany, Italy, San Gimignano, a UNESCO World Heritage Site, stands as a medieval jewel. Ascend the hilltop town and marvel at its towers, remnants of a time when families competed for prestige by building the tallest structure. In Provence, France, Saint-Rémy-de-Provence, once a Roman settlement, now exudes Provençal charm. Stroll along the Cours Mistral, lined with plane trees and cafes, and soak in the town's tranquil ambiance.

Preserving Traditions and Embracing Modernity

Historical towns and villages are not merely relics of the past; they are dynamic communities that have preserved their heritage while embracing modernity. Within their walls, you'll find a harmonious blend of traditional craftsmanship, vibrant arts scenes, and innovative culinary experiences.

In Giethoorn, Netherlands, a picturesque village known as the "Dutch Venice," explore the canals on a whisper boat and admire the thatched-roof houses lining the waterways. In Český Krumlov, Czech Republic, a UNESCO World Heritage Site, wander through the medieval center, with its Renaissance and Baroque architecture, and enjoy a traditional Czech meal in a cozy tavern.

Planning Your Historical Adventure

To fully immerse yourself in the charm of historical towns and villages, consider these tips when planning your journey:

- **Choose your destinations:** Research and select towns and villages that align with your interests and preferences. Consider their unique history, cultural offerings, and nearby attractions.

- **Embrace local experiences**: Immerse yourself in the local culture by attending traditional festivals, visiting artisan workshops, and sampling regional cuisine.

- **Venture beyond the main attractions:** Explore the lesser-known corners of these towns and villages, where you'll find hidden gems and authentic local interactions.

- **Learn the local language**: Even a few basic phrases will enhance your experience and demonstrate respect for the local culture.

- **Support local businesses**: Patronize local shops, restaurants, and accommodations to contribute to the sustainability of these communities.

A Journey Through History, Culture, and Community

Exploring historical towns and villages is more than just a sightseeing adventure; it's a journey through history, culture, and community. As you wander through these charming enclaves, you'll discover a world of preserved traditions, vibrant arts, and warm hospitality. Let the stories embedded within these ancient walls inspire you, and you'll leave enriched by the experience, carrying memories that will last a lifetime.

Sardinian Architecture

Sardinia, an island jewel nestled in the heart of the Mediterranean Sea, boasts a rich architectural heritage that reflects its diverse history and cultural influences. From the imposing nuraghe structures of the Bronze Age to the charming medieval villages and the elegant Baroque churches, Sardinia's architecture offers a captivating glimpse into the island's past and present.

Nuraghe: Echoes of a Bronze Age Civilization

Scattered across Sardinia's landscape stand the nuraghe, enigmatic stone towers that served as dwellings, strongholds, and religious centers for the Nuragic civilization, which flourished on the island from the Bronze Age to the Iron Age. These remarkable structures, built without mortar, showcase the Nuragic people's architectural prowess and their deep connection to the land.

Explore the UNESCO World Heritage Site of Su Nuraxi di Barumini, a remarkable nuraghe complex that provides a comprehensive understanding of these ancient structures. As you wander through its labyrinthine passages and gaze upon its imposing towers, imagine the lives of the Nuragic people who once inhabited these spaces.

Medieval Villages: A Blend of Fortifications and Charm

Sardinia's medieval villages, perched atop hills or nestled in valleys, offer a glimpse into the island's feudal past. These charming enclaves, with their cobblestone streets, timeworn architecture, and fortified walls, evoke a sense of history and tranquility.

Stroll through the narrow lanes of Castelsardo, a picturesque village perched on a cliff overlooking the Gulf of Asinara. Admire its Genoese-style towers and houses, and enjoy the panoramic views of the surrounding landscape. In Bosa, a village nestled along the Temo River, wander through the colorful streets and along the riverbank, and soak in the town's tranquil ambiance.

Baroque Churches: Masterpieces of Art and Faith

Sardinia's Baroque churches, with their ornate facades, rich interiors, and dramatic lighting, showcase the island's artistic expression during the

Baroque era. These awe-inspiring structures, often adorned with intricate sculptures and golden embellishments, stand as testaments to the island's religious fervor and architectural mastery.

Marvel at the grandeur of the Sacro Cuore di Gesù in Cagliari, a masterpiece of Sardinian Baroque architecture. Ascend the steps to the church and admire its imposing façade, and step inside to be captivated by its rich interior adorned with marble, stucco, and intricate carvings. In Sassari, explore the Cattedrale di San Nicola di Bari, a remarkable example of Sardinian Baroque style, and admire its lavishly decorated interior and the sacred relics it houses.

Modern Architecture: A Blend of Tradition and Innovation

Sardinia's contemporary architecture, while respecting the island's rich heritage, embraces modern design principles and innovative materials. These structures, often integrated with the natural landscape, showcase the island's commitment to sustainable development and its creative spirit.

In Olbia, the Stazione Marittima, designed by the renowned architect Rafael Moneo, seamlessly blends modern design with the port's industrial heritage. Along the Costa Smeralda, the White House, designed by Cini Boeri, exudes elegance and simplicity, harmonizing with the surrounding Mediterranean landscape.

Planning Your Architectural Adventure

To fully appreciate the architectural treasures of Sardinia, consider these tips when planning your journey:

- Choose your destinations: Research and select towns, villages, and cities that align with your architectural interests. Consider the specific styles and periods that pique your curiosity.

- Seek out hidden gems: Venture beyond the well-known landmarks and explore lesser-known architectural gems. Local guides and experts can point you towards hidden treasures.

- Appreciate the context: Understand the historical and cultural context of the architectural works you encounter. This will deepen your appreciation and enhance your understanding of their significance.

- Respect the sites: Be mindful of the preservation of these architectural treasures. Avoid touching or damaging any structures, and follow any guidelines or restrictions set by the site's management.

- Embrace the learning experience: Allow yourself to be inspired by the diversity and creativity of Sardinian architecture. Learn about the architects, the construction techniques, and the historical and cultural influences that shaped these structures.

Chapter 8: Sardinia for Food Enthusiasts

Sardinian Cuisine

Sardinian Ingredients and Flavors

For the food enthusiast seeking a culinary adventure, Sardinia, an island jewel in the heart of the Mediterranean Sea, offers an irresistible symphony of flavors and aromas. Sardinian cuisine, deeply rooted in the island's rich history and diverse cultural influences, is a testament to the ingenuity and passion of its people. Embark on a gastronomic journey through Sardinia, and let your taste buds be captivated by the island's unique culinary treasures.

Sardinian Ingredients: A Symphony of Flavors

Sardinian cuisine is a harmonious blend of fresh, locally sourced ingredients, each contributing to the island's distinctive taste profile. The fertile pastures and coastal waters provide an abundance of natural produce, while the island's agricultural traditions ensure that ingredients are treated with respect and care.

Immerse yourself in the vibrant flavors of Sardinian cuisine by savoring the island's signature ingredients:

- **Carasau bread:** This thin, crispy flatbread, a staple of Sardinian cuisine, is a versatile accompaniment to meals or a delightful snack on its own.

- **Pecorino Sardo:** This hard, aged sheep's cheese, produced in Sardinia for centuries, is a key ingredient in many Sardinian dishes, adding a rich, salty flavor.

- **Cannonau grapes:** These native grapes, grown in the island's sun-drenched vineyards, produce robust, full-bodied red wines that are integral to Sardinian cuisine.

- **Wild herbs and berries:** Sardinia's diverse flora provides an abundance of wild herbs and berries, such as myrtle, juniper, and arbutus berries, which add unique flavors and aromas to dishes.

Sardinian Flavors: A Tapestry of Culinary Delights

Sardinian cuisine is a tapestry of flavors, reflecting the island's rich cultural heritage and the diverse influences of its past. From hearty peasant dishes to sophisticated seafood creations, Sardinian cuisine offers a culinary adventure that will tantalize your taste buds.

Indulge in the island's culinary delights by sampling these signature Sardinian dishes:

- **Malloreddus**: These small, shell-shaped pasta dumplings, often served in a rich meat sauce, are a staple of Sardinian cuisine.

- **Fregola**: This toasted semolina pasta, often served with seafood or vegetables, adds a unique texture and nutty flavor to dishes.

- **Porceddu arrosto:** This slow-roasted suckling pig, a traditional dish for special occasions, is a testament to Sardinian culinary mastery.

- **Seada:** This sweet ricotta fritter, often drizzled with honey, is a delightful way to end a Sardinian meal.

A Culinary Adventure Awaits

Sardinian cuisine is more than just food; it's a cultural expression, a celebration of the island's unique heritage and flavors. Whether you're savoring a hearty dish in a traditional trattoria or enjoying a gourmet meal in an elegant restaurant, Sardinian cuisine will captivate your senses and leave you with unforgettable memories.

So, pack your appetite and embark on a culinary adventure through Sardinia. Let the island's vibrant flavors and aromas guide you as you discover the secrets of Sardinian cuisine, a symphony of tastes that will linger long after your journey ends.

Regional Specialties

Regional specialties are unique dishes or products that are associated with a particular region or area. They often reflect the local ingredients, culture, and traditions of the region. Regional specialties can be a source of pride for local residents and can attract visitors from other parts of the world.

Here are some examples of regional specialties from around the world:

- **Italy**: Pizza Napoletana from Naples, Tiramisu from Veneto, Bistecca alla Fiorentina from Tuscany, Lasagna from Emilia-Romagna

- **France**: Crêpes from Brittany, Boeuf bourguignon from Burgundy, Coq au vin from Alsace, Soufflé from Lorraine

- **Spain**: Paella from Valencia, Jamón ibérico from Andalusia, Gazpacho from Andalusia, Tortilla de patatas from Castile and León

- **Mexico**: Mole poblano from Puebla, Tacos al pastor from Mexico City, Guacamole from various regions, Chiles en nogada from Puebla

- **China**: Peking duck from Beijing, Xiaolongbao from Shanghai, Char siu from Hong Kong, Kung pao chicken from Sichuan

- **India**: Butter chicken from Punjab, Tandoori chicken from North India, Biryani from various regions, Dosa from South India

- **Japan**: Sushi from various regions, Ramen from various regions, Tempura from various regions, Matcha from Uji

- **Greece**: Moussaka from various regions, Souvlaki from various regions, Baklava from various regions, Greek salad from various regions

- **Thailand**: Pad thai from various regions, Tom yum soup from various regions, Som tam from various regions, Khao soi from Chiang Mai

- **Vietnam**: Phở from Hanoi, Bánh mì from Ho Chi Minh City, Gỏi cuốn from various regions, Cà phê sữa đá from Vietnam

These are just a few examples of the many regional specialties that can be found around the world. Each region has its own unique dishes and products that reflect its local culture and heritage.

Markets and Food Tours

Markets and food tours are a great way to experience the local culture and cuisine of a place. Markets are where locals go to buy fresh produce, meat, seafood, and other food items. Food tours are guided tours that take visitors to different restaurants and food stalls to try a variety of local dishes.

Markets

Markets are a vibrant and colorful part of everyday life in many countries. They are a great place to find fresh, local produce, meat, seafood, and other food items. Markets are also a great place to try local street food and snacks.

Some of the most famous markets in the world include:

- Chatuchak Weekend Market in Bangkok, Thailand: This is the largest weekend market in the world, with over 15,000 stalls selling everything from clothes and souvenirs to food and drinks.

- La Boqueria Market in Barcelona, Spain: This is a large indoor market selling fresh produce, meat, seafood, and other food items. There are also many tapas bars and restaurants in the market where you can try local dishes.

- Tsukiji Fish Market in Tokyo, Japan: This is the largest fish market in the world, and it is a must-visit for any food lover. The market is open to the public from 5am to 9am, and it is a fascinating sight to see.

Food Tours

Food tours are a great way to try a variety of local dishes and learn about the local cuisine. Food tours are typically guided by a local who knows the best places to eat.

Some of the most popular food tours in the world include:

- New York Pizza Tour: This tour takes visitors to some of the best pizzerias in New York City.

- Tokyo Sushi Tour: This tour takes visitors to some of the best sushi restaurants in Tokyo.

- Rome Pasta Tour: This tour takes visitors to some of the best pasta restaurants in Rome.

Tips for Visiting Markets and Taking Food Tours

Here are some tips for visiting markets and taking food tours:

- Be prepared to bargain: Bargaining is common in many markets, so be prepared to bargain for a good price.

- Try new things: Don't be afraid to try new foods and drinks. Markets are a great place to try local specialties that you may not be able to find anywhere else.

- Be respectful: Markets and food stalls are often family-run businesses, so be respectful of the vendors and their customers.

- Take your time: Markets are a great place to wander around and soak up the atmosphere. Don't rush through it.

- Enjoy yourself: Markets and food tours are a great way to experience the local culture and cuisine. So relax, have fun, and enjoy the experience.

Dining Recommendations

Fine Dining

Sardinia is an island in the Mediterranean Sea that is known for its stunning beaches, crystal-clear waters, and delicious food. If you are a first-time traveler to Sardinia, here are a few fine dining restaurants that you should not miss:

- **Dal Corsaro in Cagliari:** This restaurant is located in a beautiful old building with a terrace that overlooks the sea. The menu features traditional Sardinian dishes made with fresh, local ingredients.

- **La Sponda in Porto Cervo:** This restaurant is located in the heart of the Costa Smeralda, and it offers stunning views of the Mediterranean Sea. The menu features modern Italian cuisine with a Sardinian twist.

- **Il Refettorio in Cagliari:** This restaurant is located in a former church, and it offers a unique dining experience. The menu features traditional Sardinian dishes with a modern twist.

- **Su Gologone in Oliena:** This restaurant is located in the heart of Sardinia, and it offers a traditional Sardinian dining experience. The menu features dishes such as malloreddus alla campidanese (pasta with sausage and tomato sauce) and porceddu arrosto (roasted suckling pig).

- **Trattoria Lillicu in Cagliari:** This restaurant is located in the historic center of Cagliari, and it offers a traditional Sardinian dining experience. The menu features dishes such as spaghetti ai ricci di mare (spaghetti with sea urchin) and fregola con la bottarga (fregola with mullet roe).

Here are some tips for enjoying fine dining in Sardinia:

- **Make reservations in advance**: Fine dining restaurants in Sardinia are often booked up weeks or even months in advance, so it is important to make reservations in advance.

- **Dress appropriately:** Fine dining restaurants in Sardinia have a dress code, so it is important to dress appropriately. Men should wear a jacket and tie, and women should wear a dress or skirt.

- **Be prepared to spend money:** Fine dining restaurants in Sardinia are expensive, so be prepared to spend a significant amount of money on your meal.

- **Savor the experience**: Fine dining is not just about eating food; it is also about experiencing the atmosphere and the service. So take your time, savor your meal, and enjoy the experience.

Here are some specific recommendations for fine dining restaurants in Sardinia for first-time travelers:

- **Dal Corsaro in Cagliari:** This restaurant is a great place to try traditional Sardinian dishes such as malloreddus alla campidanese and porceddu arrosto. The restaurant also has a wide selection of Sardinian wines.

- **La Sponda in Porto Cervo**: This restaurant is a great place to try modern Italian cuisine with a Sardinian twist. The restaurant also has a stunning terrace with views of the Mediterranean Sea.

- **Il Refettorio in Cagliari:** This restaurant is a great place to try a unique dining experience in a former church. The restaurant also has a wine cellar with a wide selection of Sardinian wines.

- **Su Gologone in Oliena**: This restaurant is a great place to try a traditional Sardinian dining experience in the heart of the island. The restaurant also has a bakery where you can buy traditional Sardinian breads and pastries.

- **Trattoria Lillicu in Cagliari**: This restaurant is a great place to try a traditional Sardinian dining experience in the historic center of Cagliari. The restaurant also has a wide selection of Sardinian wines.

Local Eateries and Pizzerias

Sardinia is an island in the Mediterranean Sea that is known for its stunning beaches, crystal-clear waters, and delicious food. If you are looking for a taste of the real Sardinia, be sure to check out some of the local eateries and pizzerias.

Here are a few of my favorites:

- **Trattoria Lillicu in Cagliari:** This traditional Sardinian restaurant is located in the heart of the city's historic center. The menu features a wide variety of Sardinian dishes, including pasta with sea urchin, fregola with mullet roe, and roasted suckling pig.

- **Sa Scolla in Cagliari:** This pizzeria is known for its wood-fired pizzas made with fresh, local ingredients. The menu also features a variety of other Sardinian dishes, such as pasta and seafood.

- **Pizzeria Framento in Cagliari**: This pizzeria is another great place to try wood-fired pizzas. The menu features a variety of traditional and creative pizzas, as well as a selection of Sardinian wines.

- **Agriturismo Sa Mandra in Selargius:** This agriturismo, or farmhouse restaurant, is located in the countryside just outside of Cagliari. The menu features traditional Sardinian dishes made with fresh, seasonal ingredients. The restaurant also has a beautiful terrace with views of the surrounding countryside.

- **Bar Trattoria da Mario in Bosa**: This restaurant is located in the picturesque town of Bosa, on the west coast of Sardinia. The menu features a variety of traditional Sardinian dishes, including seafood, pasta, and meats. The restaurant also has a terrace with views of the Temo River.

- **Trattoria Su Nuraghe in Alghero**: This restaurant is located in the historic center of Alghero, a Catalan-speaking town on the northwest coast of Sardinia. The menu features a variety of traditional Sardinian dishes, as well as some Catalan-inspired dishes.

- **Pizzeria Sa Capannizza in Castelsardo**: This pizzeria is located in the picturesque village of Castelsardo, on the northwest coast of Sardinia. The pizzeria is known for its wood-fired pizzas made with fresh, local ingredients.

- **Agriturismo Mannois in Olbia:** This agriturismo is located in the countryside just outside of Olbia, in the northeast of Sardinia. The menu features traditional Sardinian dishes made with fresh, seasonal ingredients. The restaurant also has a beautiful terrace with views of the surrounding countryside.

- **Trattoria da Nicolo in Arzachena:** This restaurant is located in the town of Arzachena, on the Costa Smeralda, in the northeast of Sardinia. The menu features a variety of traditional Sardinian dishes, as well as some seafood dishes.

- **Pizzeria La Scialuppa in Palau:** This pizzeria is located in the town of Palau, on the Costa Smeralda. The pizzeria is known for its wood-fired pizzas made with fresh, local ingredients.

These are just a few of the many great local eateries and pizzerias in Sardinia. With so many options to choose from, you are sure to find a place to enjoy a delicious and authentic Sardinian meal.

Street Food

Sardinia is an island in the Mediterranean Sea known for its stunning beaches, crystal-clear waters, and delicious food. While the island's fine dining restaurants are world-class, its street food scene is equally impressive.

From savory pastries to sweet treats, Sardinian Street food offers a taste of the island's rich culinary heritage and diverse flavors. Here are some of the most popular Sardinian Street foods to try:

- **Seadas**: These sweet ricotta fritters are a Sardinian classic. They are typically filled with fresh ricotta cheese, honey, and lemon zest, and then deep-fried. Seadas are often served with a drizzle of honey or powdered sugar.

- **Culurgiones**: These savory dumplings are made with a thin pasta dough that is filled with a mixture of pecorino cheese, ricotta cheese, and fresh herbs. Culurgiones are typically boiled and then served with a simple tomato sauce.

- **Panadas**: These savory pies are made with a flaky pastry crust that is filled with a variety of ingredients, such as meat, fish, vegetables, and cheese. Panadas are typically baked in a wood-fired oven and served hot.

- **Arrosticini**: These skewered and grilled lamb or pork skewers are a popular Sardinian street food. Arrosticini are typically served with a side of grilled vegetables or bread.

- **Porceddu arrosto:** This roasted suckling pig is a traditional Sardinian dish that is often served at festivals and special occasions. Procedure arrosto is typically roasted over a wood fire and served with a side of potatoes and vegetables.

- **Fichi d'India**: These prickly pear cacti are a popular Sardinian street food. The fruit of the prickly pear cactus is sweet and juicy, and it is often eaten fresh or used to make jams and syrups.

- **Gelato:** No trip to Sardinia would be complete without trying the island's famous gelato. Sardinian gelato is made with fresh, local ingredients and comes in a variety of flavors, including pistachio, stracciatella, and nocciola.

Where to find Sardinian Street food

Sardinian street food can be found all over the island, from small villages to large cities. Here are a few tips for finding the best Sardinian Street food:

- Look for food stalls and carts in popular tourist areas.

- Ask your hotel concierge or local tourism office for recommendations.

- Follow your nose! The best Sardinian Street food is often found where the locals are eating.

Tips for enjoying Sardinian Street food

- Be adventurous and try new things. Sardinian street food offers a wide variety of flavors and textures, so don't be afraid to try something new.

- Take your time and savor the experience. Sardinian street food is meant to be enjoyed, so take your time and savor the delicious flavors.

- Don't forget to try the gelato! Sardinian gelato is world-famous, so don't miss out on the opportunity to try some of the best gelato in the world.

Sardinian street food is a delicious and authentic way to experience the island's unique culinary culture. With so many different options to choose from, you are sure to find something to your taste. Whether you are looking for a quick snack or a hearty meal, Sardinian Street food has something to offer everyone.

Sardinian Desserts and Sweets

Sardinia, an island jewel nestled in the heart of the Mediterranean Sea, is renowned for its pristine beaches, turquoise waters, and rugged landscapes. But beyond its natural beauty, Sardinia also boasts a rich culinary heritage, with desserts and sweets playing a starring role.

From delicate pastries to decadent cakes, Sardinian desserts and sweets are a testament to the island's unique cultural influences and its abundance of fresh, local ingredients. Here are some of the most popular Sardinian desserts and sweets to try:

- Seadas: These deep-fried ricotta fritters are Sardinia's signature dessert. Filled with a mixture of fresh ricotta cheese, honey, and lemon zest, seadas are typically served with a drizzle of honey or powdered sugar.

- Pardulas: These small, tart-shaped pastries are filled with a sweet ricotta cheese mixture and topped with a lattice of pastry dough. Pardulas are often flavored with lemon zest, orange zest, and vanilla extract.

- Papassini: These delicate almond biscuits are made with a combination of sweet and bitter almonds, sugar, egg whites, and lemon zest. Papassini are typically served with coffee or tea.

- Amaretti Sardi: These chewy almond cookies are made with a mixture of sweet and bitter almonds, sugar, and egg whites. Amaretti Sardi are often flavored with lemon zest, orange zest, and vanilla extract.

- Aranzada: This candied orange peel confiserie is made with strips of orange peel that are simmered in sugar syrup until candied. Aranzada is often served as a sweet treat or used as a decoration for cakes and other desserts.

- Sospiri di Ozieri: These light and airy almond cookies are made with a mixture of sweet and bitter almonds, sugar, and egg whites. Sospiri di Ozieri are often flavored with lemon zest, orange zest, and vanilla extract.

- Candelaus: These sweet almond paste candies are filled with a mixture of almonds, orange blossom water, and icing. Candelaus are often shaped into small animals or flowers.

- Caschettas: These small, half-moon-shaped pastries are filled with a sweet ricotta cheese mixture and topped with a powdered sugar glaze. Caschettas are often flavored with lemon zest, orange zest, and vanilla extract.

- Tiliccas: These thin, delicate wafers are made with a mixture of flour, water, and olive oil. Tiliccas are often filled with a sweet ricotta cheese mixture or a savory filling, such as sausage or vegetables.

- Pistoccus: These small, round cakes are made with a mixture of flour, sugar, and eggs. Pistoccus are often flavored with lemon zest, orange zest, and vanilla extract.

- Zippulas: These fried dough fritters are typically served during the Christmas season. Zippulas are often dusted with powdered sugar or drizzled with honey.

Where to find Sardinian desserts and sweets

Sardinian desserts and sweets can be found all over the island, from small villages to large cities. Here are a few tips for finding the best Sardinian desserts and sweets:

- Look for pastry shops and cafes in popular tourist areas.

- Ask your hotel concierge or local tourism office for recommendations.

- Follow your sweet tooth! The best Sardinian desserts and sweets are often found where the locals are buying them.

Tips for enjoying Sardinian desserts and sweets

- Pair Sardinian desserts and sweets with a glass of Sardinian wine. The island's sweet wines, such as Moscato di Cagliari and Vernaccia di Oristano, are the perfect complement to Sardinian desserts and sweets.

- Share Sardinian desserts and sweets with friends and family. Sardinian desserts and sweets are meant to be enjoyed and shared.

So gather your loved ones and savor a taste of Sardinian culinary

Chapter 9: Practical Tips for Travelers

Accommodations and Lodging

Hotels, Resorts, and Agriturismos

Sardinia, an island jewel nestled in the heart of the Mediterranean Sea, offers a diverse range of accommodation options, from luxurious hotels and resorts to charming agriturismos (farmhouse inns). Whether you are seeking a romantic getaway, a family-friendly vacation, or an adventure-filled escape, you are sure to find the perfect place to stay in Sardinia.

Hotels

Sardinia's hotels offer a range of amenities and services, from world-class spas and restaurants to private pools and stunning beachfront locations. Here are a few of the most highly-rated hotels in Sardinia:

- Hotel Cala di Volpe: Located on the Costa Smeralda, Hotel Cala di Volpe is a luxurious hotel with its own private beach, marina, and golf course. The hotel offers a range of amenities and services, including a spa, fitness center, and several restaurants.

- Forte Village Resort: Located on the south coast of Sardinia, Forte Village Resort is a family-friendly resort with seven hotels, a variety of restaurants, and a wide range of activities for kids of all ages. The resort also has its own private beach and marina.

- Is Molas Resort: Located on the southwestern coast of Sardinia, Is Molas Resort is a luxury resort with its own private beach, golf course, and spa. The resort also offers a variety of restaurants and bars.

Resorts

Sardinia's resorts offer a more all-inclusive experience, with everything you need for a relaxing and enjoyable vacation under one roof. Here are a few of the most popular resorts in Sardinia:

- Chia Laguna: Located on the south coast of Sardinia, Chia Laguna is a resort complex with four hotels, a variety of restaurants, and a wide range of activities for guests of all ages. The resort also has its own private beach and marina.

- **Resort Valle dell'Erica**: Located on the Costa Smeralda, Resort Valle dell'Erica is a luxury resort with its own private beach, golf course, and spa. The resort also offers a variety of restaurants and bars.

- **Arbatax Park Resort:** Located on the east coast of Sardinia, Arbatax Park Resort is a family-friendly resort with three hotels, a variety of restaurants, and a wide range of activities for kids of all ages. The resort also has its own private beach.

Agriturismos

Sardinia's agriturismos offer a unique and authentic accommodation experience. These farmhouse inns are often located in rural areas and offer guests the opportunity to experience Sardinian culture and cuisine firsthand. Here are a few of the most highly-rated agriturismos in Sardinia:

- **Agriturismo Su Nuraghe:** Located in the countryside near Cagliari, Agriturismo Su

Nuraghe offers a traditional Sardinian experience. The agriturismo has a restaurant that serves regional dishes, and guests can also participate in activities such as cooking classes and wine tastings.

- **Agriturismo Sa Mandra:** Located in the countryside near Selargius, Agriturismo Sa Mandra offers a relaxing and peaceful getaway. The agriturismo has a restaurant that serves traditional Sardinian dishes, and guests can also enjoy the swimming pool and gardens.

- **Agriturismo Mannois:** Located in the countryside near Olbia, Agriturismo Mannois offers a family-friendly accommodation experience. The agriturismo has a restaurant that serves traditional Sardinian dishes, and guests can also participate in activities such as horseback riding and swimming.

Tips for Choosing Accommodation in Sardinia

When choosing accommodation in Sardinia, there are a few factors to keep in mind:

- **Budget:** Sardinia has a wide range of accommodation options to suit all budgets. From budget-friendly hostels to luxury hotels, you are sure to find something that fits your needs.

- **Location:** Sardinia is a large island, so it is important to consider where you want to stay. If you are looking for a beach vacation, you will want to choose accommodation near the coast. If you are interested in exploring Sardinia's culture and history, you may want to choose accommodation in one of the island's villages or towns.

- **Amenities:** Consider what amenities are important to you when choosing accommodation in Sardinia. Some hotels and resorts offer spas, fitness centers, and other amenities, while agriturismos tend to offer a more rustic experience.

Sardinia offers a diverse range of accommodation options, from

Booking Accommodations

Sardinia is a beautiful island in the Mediterranean Sea with a lot to offer visitors. From its stunning beaches to its charming villages, there is something for everyone in Sardinia. However, with so many different accommodation options available, it can be difficult to know where to start.

In this guide, I will share my experience of booking accommodations in Sardinia and provide some tips to help you choose the right place to stay.

When to Book

Sardinia is a popular tourist destination, so it is important to book your accommodation well in advance, especially if you are traveling during peak season (June-August). If you are traveling on a budget, you may be able to find some good deals on last-minute accommodation, but it is always best to book early to avoid disappointment.

Where to Book

There are a number of different ways to book accommodations in Sardinia. You can book directly through the hotel or resort's website, or you can use a booking website such as Expedia or Booking.com. I personally prefer to book directly through the hotel or resort's website, as this often gives you the best price and the most flexibility.

Types of Accommodations

There are a variety of different accommodation options available in Sardinia, from hotels and resorts to agriturismos (farmhouse inns) and villas. The type of accommodation you choose will depend on your budget, your interests, and the type of vacation you are looking for.

Hotels and Resorts

Hotels and resorts offer the widest range of amenities and services, such as swimming pools, restaurants, and spas. They are also the most expensive type of accommodation in Sardinia.

Agriturismos

Agriturismos are a great option for travelers who are looking for a more authentic Sardinian experience. These farmhouse inns are often located in rural areas and offer guests the opportunity to sample traditional Sardinian cuisine and learn about Sardinian culture.

Villas

Villas are a good option for travelers who are looking for more space and privacy. Villas can be rented for a week or longer, and they often come with their own private pools and gardens.

My Experience

When I was planning my trip to Sardinia, I decided to book a stay at an agriturismo. I wanted to experience the island's culture and cuisine firsthand, and I thought that an agriturismo would be the perfect place to do that.

I chose to stay at Agriturismo Su Nuraghe, which is located in the countryside near Cagliari. The agriturismo is owned and operated by a Sardinian family, and they were very welcoming and friendly.

My room was spacious and comfortable, and it had a balcony with stunning views of the surrounding countryside. The agriturismo also has a restaurant that serves traditional Sardinian dishes, and the food was delicious.

I had a wonderful time at Agriturismo Su Nuraghe, and I would highly recommend it to anyone looking for an authentic Sardinian experience.

Tips for Booking Accommodations in Sardinia

Here are a few tips to help you book accommodations in Sardinia:

- Book well in advance, especially if you are traveling during peak season.

- Compare prices from different websites before you book.

- Read reviews of hotels, resorts, and agriturismos before you book.

- Consider the location of the accommodation when booking.

- Make sure that the accommodation has the amenities and services that you need.

Booking accommodations in Sardinia is a straightforward process, but it is important to plan ahead and to choose the right type of accommodation for your needs. I hope that this guide has been helpful, and I wish you a wonderful vacation in Sardinia!

Accommodation Etiquette

When staying at a hotel, resort, or other type of accommodation, it is important to be respectful of the property and the staff. Here are a few tips for following accommodation etiquette:

- Check in and out on time. If you are arriving late or checking out early, be sure to notify the hotel or resort in advance.

- Be respectful of other guests. This means keeping the noise down, especially at night. It also means being mindful of your personal space and not taking up too much space in common areas.

- Keep your room clean and tidy. When you leave your room for the day, be sure to make the bed, empty the trash, and close the curtains or blinds.

- Tip the staff. Tipping is customary for hotel and resort staff, such as housekeepers, bellhops, and concierge. A tip of 1-2 euros per night for housekeepers is generally considered appropriate.

- Take care of the property. This means not damaging the furniture or fixtures and not leaving any trash behind.

Here are some additional tips for following accommodation etiquette:

- Be quiet in the hallways and common areas. This is especially important at night when other guests are trying to sleep.

- Don't take food or drinks from the common areas to your room. If you want to eat or drink in your room, order it from the hotel or resort's restaurant or bar.

- Don't smoke in your room, unless it is specifically designated as a smoking room.

- Don't leave your belongings unattended in common areas. This includes things like towels, laptops, and phones.

- If you have any problems with your room or the property, be sure to notify the hotel or resort staff immediately.

Here are some specific tips for accommodation etiquette in different types of accommodations:

Hotels

- When you arrive at the hotel, go to the front desk to check in. The front desk staff will assign you a room and give you a key.

- If you have any luggage, the bellhops can help you bring it to your room.

- Your room will be cleaned daily by the housekeeping staff. If you have any special requests, such as extra towels or pillows, be sure to let the housekeeping staff know.

- If you are staying at a hotel with a pool or other amenities, be sure to follow the posted rules. For example, there may be rules about noise levels or dress code.

Resorts

- Resorts typically offer more amenities and services than hotels. This may include things like a spa, golf course, or kids' club.

- When you arrive at the resort, go to the front desk to check in. The front desk staff will assign you a room and give you a key.

- Your room will be cleaned daily by the housekeeping staff. If you have any special requests, such as extra towels or pillows, be sure to let the housekeeping staff know.

- Resorts typically have a more casual dress code than hotels. However, it is still important to be respectful of other guests and staff.

Agriturismos

- Agriturismos are typically smaller and more intimate than hotels and resorts. They are often located in rural areas and offer guests the opportunity to experience traditional Sardinian culture and cuisine.

- When you arrive at the agriturismo, go to the reception to check in. The reception staff will assign you a room and give you a key.

- Your room may be cleaned daily, or it may be cleaned every few days. This will vary depending on the agriturismo. If you have any special requests, such as extra towels or pillows, be sure to let the reception staff know.

- Agriturismos typically have a more relaxed atmosphere than hotels and resorts. However, it is still important to be respectful of other guests and staff.

Following accommodation etiquette is important for ensuring that everyone has a pleasant experience. By being respectful of the property and the staff, you can help to create a comfortable and welcoming environment for everyone.

Alternative Stays

There's more to Sardinia than just hotels and resorts. Here are a few alternative stays to consider for your next trip:

Glamping:

Glamping, or glamorous camping, is a great way to experience the outdoors without sacrificing comfort. In Sardinia, you can find glamping sites in a variety of settings, from secluded beaches to lush forests. Some glamping sites even offer unique accommodations, such as treehouses, yurts, and safari tents.

Houseboats:

Staying on a houseboat is a unique way to explore Sardinia's coastline. You can moor your houseboat in a different cove each night, or even sail to one of the island's many offshore islands. Houseboats come in a variety of sizes and styles, so you can find one that's perfect for your needs.

Farmhouses:

Staying on a working farmhouse is a great way to experience rural Sardinian life. Many farmhouses offer accommodations to guests, and some even offer cooking classes and other activities. Staying on a farmhouse is also a great way to sample fresh, Sardinian produce.

Castles:

Sardinia is home to a number of castles, some of which are now available to rent as vacation accommodations. Staying in a castle is a truly unique experience, and it's a great way to learn about Sardinia's rich history.

Monasteries:

A few monasteries in Sardinia have been converted into hotels or guesthouses. Staying in a monastery is a peaceful and relaxing experience, and it's a great way to learn about Sardinian culture and religion.

No matter what your budget or interests are, you're sure to find an alternative stay in Sardinia that's perfect for you. So why not try something new and have an unforgettable vacation experience?

Tips for booking an alternative stay in Sardinia

- **Book in advance**: Alternative stays in Sardinia can be very popular, so it's important to book well in advance, especially if you're traveling during peak season.

- **Read reviews**: Before you book, be sure to read reviews of the alternative stay you're considering. This will help you to get an idea of what other guests have experienced and to make sure that the stay is right for you.

- **Ask questions:** If you have any questions about the alternative stay you're considering, be sure to ask the owner or manager. They will be happy to answer your questions and help you to make the best decision for your vacation.

Language and Communication

Useful Phrases and Words

Here are some useful phrases and words in Sardinian:

Greetings and common expressions

- Bonas dies - Good morning

- Bona tarde - Good afternoon
- Bona notte - Good evening/night
- Aìosu - Bye
- A menzus bìere - See you later (take care)
- Zi vidimmu - See you (Sassarese dialect)
- Nos bidimus (northern Sardinia), nos bideus (central and southern Sardinia) - See you (plural)
- Cumusta ses? - How are you?
- E tue? - And you?
- De in ue ses? - Where are you from? (singular)
- De in ue bènis? - Where are you from? (plural)
- In ue che vives? - Where do you live?
- A lu faèddas su Sardu? - Do you speak Sardinian?

- No, a lu faèddas su Sardu - No, I don't speak Sardinian

- Chistionas Sardu? - Do you speak Sardinian? (Campidanese dialect)

- No, non chistionu Sardu - No, I don't speak Sardinian (Campidanese dialect)

Food and drink

- Pane - Bread

- Vinu - Wine

- Birra - Beer

- Acqua - Water

- Casu - Cheese

- Pane carasau - Sardinian flatbread

- Porceddu arrosto - Roasted suckling pig

- Culurgiones - Sardinian dumplings

- Seadas - Sardinian fried ricotta fritters
- Gelato - Ice cream

Getting around

- Autobus - Bus
- Treno - Train
- Aeroporto - Airport
- Porto - Port
- Dove è la fermata dell'autobus? - Where is the bus stop?
- Dove è la stazione dei treni? - Where is the train station?
- Quanto costa il biglietto? - How much is the ticket?

Asking for directions

- Dove posso trovare...? - Where can I find...?

- Come posso arrivare a...? - How can I get to...?

- Sei lontano da qui? - Is it far from here?

- A sinistra - To the left

- A destra - To the right

- Dritto - Straight ahead

Other useful phrases

- Grazie - Thank you

- Prego - You're welcome

- Mi scusi - Excuse me

- Per favore - Please

- Non capisco - I don't understand

- Parla più lentamente, per favore - Please speak more slowly

- Aiuto! - Help!

Here are some additional tips for communicating in Sardinia:

- Be patient and understanding. Not everyone in Sardinia speaks English, so be patient and understanding if there is a communication barrier.

- Try to learn a few basic Sardinian phrases. This will show that you are making an effort to communicate with the locals and will be appreciated.

- Don't be afraid to ask for help. If you are lost or confused, don't be afraid to ask a local for help. Most Sardinians are friendly and helpful people.

Communication Tips

Language Resources

As a professional traveler, I have learned that communication is key to a successful trip. This is especially true when traveling to a country where you don't speak the language. Here are some language resources that I recommend for travelers in Sardinia:

Phrasebooks

A phrasebook is a great way to learn basic phrases in Sardinian. There are many different phrasebooks available, so be sure to choose one that is tailored to your needs. For example, if you are planning on spending a lot of time in Cagliari, you may want to choose a phrasebook that includes phrases specific to the city.

Dictionaries

A dictionary can be helpful for translating more complex words and phrases. There are many different dictionaries available, both online and in print. I recommend choosing a dictionary that includes both Sardinian and English.

Translation apps

Translation apps such as Google Translate and iTranslate can be helpful for translating on the go. However, it is important to keep in mind that these apps are not always accurate, so it is important to double-check any translations before using them.

Online resources

There are many online resources that can help you learn Sardinian. One of my favorite resources is the Sardinian language website at www.sardegnacultura.it. This website offers a variety of resources, including online courses, grammar lessons, and vocabulary lists.

Language schools

If you are serious about learning Sardinian, you may want to consider taking a class at a local language school. This is a great way to learn the language from a native speaker and to practice your speaking and listening skills.

Conversation partners

One of the best ways to learn Sardinian is to practice speaking it with a native speaker. You can find conversation partners online or through local language schools.

Here are some additional tips from my personal experience as a professional traveler:

- Download a Sardinian dictionary app to your phone. This will allow you to translate words and phrases on the go.

- Learn the Sardinian alphabet. This will help you to pronounce words correctly and to read basic signs.

- Don't be afraid to make mistakes. Everyone makes mistakes when they are learning a new language. The important thing is to keep practicing and to learn from your mistakes.

- Be patient and understanding. Learning a new language takes time and effort. Don't get discouraged if you don't understand everything right away.

Local Dialects

Sardinia has a rich and diverse culture, and this is reflected in its language. There are four main Sardinian dialects: Campidanese, Logudorese, Sassarese, and Gallurese. Each dialect has its own unique features and pronunciation.

Campidanese is the most widely spoken Sardinian dialect. It is spoken in the southern and central parts of the island. Campidanese is characterized by its soft consonants and its use of the definite article "su" before both masculine and feminine nouns.

Logudorese is the second most widely spoken Sardinian dialect. It is spoken in the northern and central parts of the island. Logudorese is characterized by its hard consonants and its use of the definite article "s' " before masculine nouns and "sa" before feminine nouns.

Sassarese is a Sardinian dialect that is spoken in the city of Sassari and the surrounding area. Sassarese is characterized by its use of the definite article "lu" before both masculine and feminine nouns.

Gallurese is a Sardinian dialect that is spoken in the Gallura region in the northeast of the island. Gallurese is characterized by its use of the definite article "lu" before masculine nouns and "la" before feminine nouns.

In addition to these four main dialects, there are also a number of smaller dialects and subdialects spoken in Sardinia. For example, the Tabarchino dialect is spoken in the town of Carloforte, which was founded by Ligurian fishermen in the 18th century.

Here are some examples of the different Sardinian dialects:

	A	B	C	D	E
1	English	Campidanese	Logudorese	Sassarese	Gallurese
2	Hello	Bonas die	Bonu die	Bonu die	Bonu die
3	Goodbye	Aiosu	Aiosu	Aiosu	Aiosu
4	Thank you	Grazie	Gràssias	Grazie	Grazie
5	You're welcome	Prego	Pregu	Pregu	Pregu
6	How are you?	Cumusta ses?	Comosta ses?	Comosta ses?	Comu stai?
7	I'm fine	Bènnere	Bènnere	Bènnere	Bènnere

Here are some examples of how the different Sardinian dialects are used in everyday life:

- A Campidanese speaker might say "Su pane carasau est unu pane sardu squisitu" (Campidanese: Campidanese flatbread is a delicious Sardinian bread).

- A Logudorese speaker might say "S' pane carasau est unu pane sardu squisitu" (Logudorese: Logudorese flatbread is a delicious Sardinian bread).

- A Sassarese speaker might say "Lu pane carasau est unu pane sardu squisitu" (Sassarese: Sassarese flatbread is a delicious Sardinian bread).

- A Gallurese speaker might say "Lu pane carasau est un pane sardu squisitu" (Gallurese: Gallurese flatbread is a delicious Sardinian bread).

The Sardinian dialects are an important part of the island's culture and identity. They are a living language, and they are spoken by people of all ages and social backgrounds. If you are planning a trip to Sardinia, I encourage you to learn a few basic phrases in one of the local dialects. This will help you to communicate with the locals and to experience the island's culture in a more authentic way.

Chapter 10: Sardinia Dos and Don'ts

Respect for Local Customs

Dos

- Learn a few basic Sardinian phrases. This shows that you're making an effort to connect with the locals and appreciate their culture. Even if you don't speak Sardinian fluently, knowing a few simple phrases like "hello," "goodbye," "please," and "thank you" will go a long way.

- Dress modestly, especially when visiting religious sites. Sardinians are generally conservative, so it's best to avoid wearing revealing clothing in public. When visiting churches or other religious sites, be sure to cover your shoulders and knees.

- Be respectful of Sardinian traditions. Sardinia has a rich history and culture, and its people are proud of their heritage. Be respectful of Sardinian traditions, such as the island's traditional dress, music, and food.

- Support local businesses. When you're in Sardinia, try to support local businesses as much as possible. This helps to keep the island's economy strong and preserves its unique culture.

- Be patient and understanding. Sardinians are generally friendly and helpful people, but they can also be a bit reserved at first. Be patient and understanding, and don't be afraid to ask for help if you need it.

Don'ts

- Don't be loud and obnoxious. Sardinians appreciate peace and quiet, so avoid being loud and obnoxious in public. This is especially important in small villages and rural areas.

- Don't litter or pollute the environment. Sardinians take great pride in their island's natural beauty, so don't litter or pollute the environment. Be sure to dispose of your trash properly and respect the local wildlife.

- Don't haggle with merchants. Haggling is not customary in Sardinia, so it's best to avoid haggling with merchants. If you see something you want to buy, be prepared to pay the asking price.

- Don't be critical of Sardinian culture. Sardinians are proud of their culture, so avoid being critical of it. If you have any questions or concerns, it's best to ask a local in a respectful manner.

- Don't forget to have fun! Sardinia is a beautiful island with a lot to offer visitors. Relax, enjoy the scenery, and experience the Sardinian way of life.

Here are a few specific examples of how I've shown respect for Sardinian customs during my trips to the island:

- When visiting churches, I've always covered my shoulders and knees.

- I've avoided wearing revealing clothing in public.

- I've learned a few basic Sardinian phrases, such as "hello," "goodbye," "please," and "thank you."

- I've supported local businesses by eating at local restaurants and buying souvenirs from local shops.

- I've been patient and understanding with the locals, and I've avoided being loud and obnoxious.

Environmental Responsibility

Sardinia is a beautiful island with a rich natural environment. It is home to stunning beaches, crystal-clear waters, and lush forests. However, this fragile ecosystem is at risk from a number of environmental threats, including climate change, pollution, and overdevelopment.

As visitors to Sardinia, we have a responsibility to protect the island's environment. Here are a few tips for being an environmentally responsible traveler in Sardinia:

- Reduce your waste. One of the best ways to reduce your environmental impact is to reduce your waste. Bring your own reusable water bottle, shopping bags, and utensils. Avoid using single-use plastics whenever possible.

- Dispose of your trash properly. Be sure to dispose of your trash properly in designated waste bins. Never litter or leave trash behind on beaches, in forests, or in other natural areas.

- Conserve water and energy. Sardinians are very aware of the importance of conserving water and energy, especially during the summer months. Be sure to turn off lights and water faucets when you're not using them. Take shorter showers and avoid washing clothes unnecessarily.

- Respect wildlife. Sardinia is home to a variety of unique wildlife, including wild sheep, goats, and birds. Be respectful of wildlife and avoid disturbing their habitat.

- Support sustainable businesses. When choosing where to stay, eat, and shop, look for businesses that are committed to sustainability. These businesses may use renewable energy, source local food, and recycle their waste.

Here are some specific examples of how you can be an environmentally responsible traveler in Sardinia:

- When you're at the beach, use a beach umbrella instead of a parasol. Parasols can damage the sand dunes and disrupt the nesting habits of sea turtles.

- If you're hiking in the forest, stay on designated trails. Avoid going off-trail, as this can damage the vegetation and disturb wildlife.

- If you're fishing, be sure to release any fish that you don't plan on eating. Overfishing is a major threat to Sardinia's marine environment.

- If you're staying at a hotel, ask if they have a recycling program. If not, encourage them to start one.

- When you're eating at a restaurant, order local and seasonal produce. This helps to reduce the environmental impact of food transportation.

Safety and Health Tips

Safety tips

Be aware of your surroundings and take precautions to avoid pickpocketing and other petty theft. This is especially important in crowded areas such as tourist attractions and public transportation. Here are some specific tips:

- Keep your valuables close to you at all times, such as in a front-facing backpack or inside your jacket pocket.

- Avoid carrying large amounts of cash. If you need to carry cash, keep it in a money belt or other concealed location.

- Be careful when using ATMs. Try to use ATMs in well-lit areas and be aware of your surroundings.

- If you are approached by someone asking for money or directions, be polite but firm and decline their request.

Be careful when walking at night, especially in isolated areas. Avoid walking alone at night, and if you must walk, try to stay in well-lit areas. If you are lost, ask a trusted local for help.

If you are renting a car, be aware of the local traffic laws and customs. Sardinians tend to drive aggressively, so be prepared for this. Also, be aware of the narrow roads and mountain driving conditions. Here are some specific tips:

- Obey the speed limit and traffic signs.

- Be careful when overtaking other vehicles.

- Be aware of the narrow roads and mountain driving conditions.

- If you are not comfortable driving in Sardinia, consider taking public transportation or hiring a driver.

If you are planning on hiking or camping, be sure to tell someone where you are going and when you expect to be back. Also, be prepared for changing weather conditions and bring plenty of water and food. Here are some specific tips:

- Let someone know where you are going and when you expect to be back.

- Check the weather forecast before you go and be prepared for changing weather conditions.

- Bring plenty of water and food.

- Wear appropriate clothing and footwear.

- Be aware of the local wildlife and hazards.

Health tips

Be sure to have all of your necessary vaccinations before traveling to Sardinia. This includes vaccinations for tetanus, diphtheria, measles, mumps, and rubella. You may also need to get vaccinated for hepatitis A and B, and typhoid, depending on your travel itinerary. You can get vaccinated at a travel clinic or your primary care doctor.

Drink bottled water and avoid eating raw fruits and vegetables to reduce your risk of getting sick. Sardinian tap water is generally safe to drink, but it is always best to err on the side of caution and drink bottled water. Avoid eating raw fruits and vegetables, as they may be contaminated with bacteria.

Use sunscreen and wear protective clothing to protect yourself from the sun. Sardinia has a Mediterranean climate, which means that the sun can be very strong, especially in the summer months. Be sure to use sunscreen with an SPF of 30 or higher and wear protective clothing, such as a hat and sunglasses.

Be aware of the signs and symptoms of heat stroke and dehydration, and take steps to avoid these conditions. Heat stroke and dehydration are serious medical conditions that can be fatal. Be sure to stay hydrated by drinking plenty of fluids, and avoid strenuous activity during the hottest part of the day. If you experience any of the following symptoms, seek medical attention immediately: headache, dizziness, nausea, vomiting, confusion, and loss of consciousness.

If you do get sick, be sure to see a doctor promptly. Sardinian healthcare system is good, and you will be able to receive quality medical care if you need it. Be sure to bring your travel insurance information with you, so that you can be reimbursed for any medical expenses.

Pack a first-aid kit and any necessary medications when you travel. This will ensure that you have the necessary supplies on hand if you need them.

Bring a copy of your passport and other important documents with you, but leave the originals in a safe place at your accommodation. This will protect your documents in case they are lost or stolen.

Learn a few basic Sardinian phrases, such as "hello," "goodbye," "please," and "thank you." This will show that you are making an effort to communicate with the locals and will be appreciated.

Be respectful of Sardinian culture and customs. Sardinians are a proud people with a rich culture. Be respectful of their traditions and customs, and avoid doing anything that could be considered offensive.

By following these safety and health tips, you can help to ensure that you have a safe and healthy trip to Sardinia. Sardinia is a beautiful island with a lot to offer visitors, but it is

Souvenirs and Mementos

Sardinia is a beautiful island with a rich culture, and there are many souvenirs and mementos that you can bring home to remember your trip. Here are a few ideas:

Food and drink: Sardinia is known for its delicious food and drink, so be sure to try some of the local specialties and bring some home with you. Some popular food souvenirs include:

- **Pane carasau:** A traditional Sardinian flatbread made from durum wheat semolina. It is thin and crispy, and can be eaten plain or with toppings such as cheese, olives, and tomatoes.

- **Formaggio pecorino:** A sheep's milk cheese that is aged for several months. It has a strong, nutty flavor and is often used in Sardinian cooking.

- **Botarga:** A dried and salted tuna roe that is grated over pasta dishes or used as a condiment.

- **Miele di corbezzolo**: A honey made from the nectar of the strawberry tree. It has a dark color and a rich, sweet flavor.

- **Cannonau:** A red wine that is produced in Sardinia. It has a full-bodied flavor and is often paired with meats and cheeses.

Crafts: Sardinia has a long tradition of craftsmanship, and there are many unique and beautiful crafts that you can purchase as souvenirs. Some popular craft souvenirs include:

- **Cesteria:** Sardinian baskets are made from a variety of materials, including reeds, rushes, and straw. They are often decorated with intricate patterns and are prized for their beauty and durability.

- **Tessitura:** Sardinian textiles are made from a variety of materials, including wool, linen, and cotton. They are often decorated with traditional Sardinian motifs and are prized for their quality and craftsmanship.

- **Ceramica:** Sardinian ceramics are known for their bright colors and bold designs. They are often made from local clay and are fired in wood-fired kilns.

- **Filigrana:** Sardinian filigree jewelry is made from delicate silver threads that are woven into intricate patterns. It is a beautiful and traditional craft that has been passed down from generation to generation.

Art: Sardinia has a rich artistic tradition, and there are many beautiful paintings, sculptures, and other works of art that you can purchase as souvenirs. Some popular art souvenirs include:

- Maschere: Sardinian masks are made from wood or paper and are used in traditional festivals and carnivals. They are often decorated with elaborate designs and are prized for their cultural significance.

- **Tappeti:** Sardinian carpets are made from a variety of materials, including wool, linen, and cotton. They are often decorated with traditional Sardinian motifs and are prized for their quality and craftsmanship.

- **Quadri:** Sardinian paintings often depict scenes from Sardinian life or the island's natural beauty. They are a beautiful and unique way to remember your trip to Sardinia.

No matter what your budget is, you are sure to find souvenirs and mementos in Sardinia that you will cherish for years to come. Be sure to take your time shopping and browse the many different stalls and shops to find the perfect items to take home.

ENJOY YOUR TRIP

Printed in Great Britain
by Amazon